Teaching Arabic as a Heritage Language

Teaching Arabic as a Heritage Language is a practical guide to Arabic pedagogy for Heritage Language Learners of Arabic.

Exploring the teaching of Arabic as a foreign language (TAFL) in North America and Europe, it covers sociocultural topics such as diglossia and religion alongside theoretical approaches to Heritage Language Learning. It also provides a new and detailed definition of the heritage language learner (HLL) of Arabic. The role of the professor and the material are explored to ensure a successful learning experience. The latest advances in HLL are considered together with the recent and recommended changes in classroom practice, giving rise to the recognition of the individual needs of heritage learners.

This is an indispensable resource for instructors, researchers, and students in the fields of TAFL and TASOL, as well as linguists interested in Arabic language learning and teaching.

Rasha ElHawari is a Senior Lecturer of Arabic and the Coordinator for the Semitic Languages Program at Concordia University, Montreal, Canada. She has extensive experience in TAFL and teaching Arabic immersion programs.

Teaching Arabic as a Heritage Language

Rasha ElHawari

Routledge
Taylor & Francis Group
LONDON AND NEW YORK

First published 2021
by Routledge
2 Park Square, Milton Park, Abingdon, Oxon OX14 4RN

and by Routledge
52 Vanderbilt Avenue, New York, NY 10017

Routledge is an imprint of the Taylor & Francis Group, an informa business

© 2021 Rasha ElHawari

The right of Rasha ElHawari to be identified as author of this work has been asserted by her in accordance with sections 77 and 78 of the Copyright, Designs and Patents Act 1988.

All rights reserved. No part of this book may be reprinted or reproduced or utilised in any form or by any electronic, mechanical, or other means, now known or hereafter invented, including photocopying and recording, or in any information storage or retrieval system, without permission in writing from the publishers.

Trademark notice: Product or corporate names may be trademarks or registered trademarks, and are used only for identification and explanation without intent to infringe.

British Library Cataloguing-in-Publication Data
A catalogue record for this book is available from the British Library

Library of Congress Cataloging-in-Publication Data
A catalog record has been requested for this book

ISBN: 978-1-138-49933-1 (hbk)
ISBN: 978-1-138-49940-9 (pbk)
ISBN: 978-1-351-01467-0 (ebk)

Typeset in Times New Roman
by Deanta Global Publishing Services, Chennai, India

Contents

List of illustrations ix
Preface x
Acknowledgments xi
List of abbreviations in alphabetical order xii
Introduction xiii
Readership xv

PART 1
Arabic as a heritage language 1

1 What is a heritage language? 3

1.0 Introduction 3
1.1 A definition of heritage language 3
  1.1.1 Indigenous heritage languages 5
  1.1.2 Colonial heritage languages 6
  1.1.3 Immigrant heritage languages 6
  1.1.4 Ancestral heritage languages 6
  1.1.5 Minority languages – Canada 7
1.2 Heritage languages and language policy in the United States 7
  1.2.1 Heritage languages in the United States – Spanish 9
  1.2.2 Heritage languages in the United States – American-born Africans 9
1.3 Heritage languages and language policy in Canada 10
  1.3.1 Heritage languages in the United States and Canada – Arabic 11
1.4 Heritage languages in Europe 12
Notes 14
Bibliography 14
Additional References 15

2 Arabic language(s) in the Arab World — 17

2.0 Introduction 17
2.1 Arabic: A Semitic language 18
2.2 Diglossia 19
2.3 Levels of Arabic and Arabic usage 21
2.4 Arabic dialects 23
2.5 Arabic in the Arab World 25
2.6 Arabic language in Israel: A special status 25
2.7 Minority languages in the Arab World 26
Notes 28
Bibliography 28
Additional References 29

3 Arabic beyond the Arab World — 31

3.0 Introduction 31
3.1 Arabic and religion 31
3.2 Arabic language and Muslim/non-Arab communities 34
    3.2.1 Arabic in Africa: Nigeria 34
    3.2.2 Arabic in Asia: Indonesia 36
3.3 Arabic language and non-Muslim/non-Arab communities 37
    3.3.1 Arabic in Malta: Semitic meets Romance 37
    3.3.2 Arabic in Ethiopia 38
3.4 Arabic in immigrant communities 38
    3.4.1 Arabic immigrant communities in North America 39
    3.4.2 Arabic immigrant communities in Europe: Denmark 41
3.5 Arabic as a language in the West 42
    3.5.1 Arabic words in English in recent times 44
    3.5.2 Arabic proper names in the West 45
Notes 46
Bibliography 46
Additional References 48

PART 2
Heritage language learning pedagogy — 49

4 Heritage language learners and assessment of Arabic language proficiency — 51

4.0 Introduction 51
4.1 Standard proficiency tests 51

4.2 American Council of Teaching Foreign Languages 52
4.3 Common European Framework of Reference for Languages (CEFR) 58
4.4 Other Arabic proficiency tests 61
    4.4.1 The Interagency Language Roundtable Test (ILR) 61
    4.4.2 Al-Arabiyya Test 62
4.5 Proficiency tests and the heritage language learner 63
4.6 Language placement and the heritage language learner 64
Notes 66
Bibliography 66
Additional References 67

5 The heritage language learner of Arabic 69

5.0 Introduction 69
5.1 The language learner of Arabic 69
5.2 Defining the heritage language learner of Arabic 72
    5.2.1 Two different subgroups of HLLs of Arabic: G-HLL and M-HLL 74
5.3 Family and the heritage language learner 79
5.4 Understanding different levels of the HLL 80
    5.4.1 G-HLL beginner dialect, beginner MSA 82
    5.4.2 G-HLL intermediate dialect, beginner MSA 83
    5.4.3 G-HLL advanced dialect speaker, beginner MSA 84
    5.4.4 M-HLL, writes Arabic script 85
Notes 86
Bibliography 86
Additional References 87

6 The heritage language learner and the Arabic language classroom 88

6.0 Introduction 88
6.1 The language professor and the HLL 88
6.2 Classroom diversity and Arabic language learning strategies 92
6.3 The HLL and non-HLL in the classroom 93
    6.3.1 The HLL and Arabic varieties in the classroom 95
6.4 The HLL and knowledge of Arabic language and culture 95
6.5 The HLL and the Arabic coursebook 97
6.6 University undergraduate curricula 98
    6.6.1 Description of an Arabic program 99
    6.6.2 Curriculum changes and administration 101

6.7 Study-abroad programs and the HLL 102
6.8 The heritage language learner of Arabic: A summary 105
Bibliography 106
Additional References 107

Index 109

Illustrations

Figures

2.1	Chart showing social and geographical representation of the Arabic language	25
3.1	MENA immigrant population in the US between 1980 and 2016	40
4.1	ACTFL classification of levels of proficiency of Arabic 2012 guidelines (actfl.org)	53
4.2	CEFR language proficiency levels (Council of Europe Portal, 2019)	59
4.3	The ILR scale (Herzog, History of the ILR Scale)	62

Tables

4.1	Arabic writing-specific annotations from ACTFL Arabic guidelines (ACTFL, 2012)	55
4.2	Arabic speaking-specific annotations from ACTFL Arabic guidelines (ACTFL, 2012)	56
4.3	Common reference levels: Global scale (Council of Europe, 2001, p. 24)	60
5.1	Adapted from MLA enrollment survey – 2016 enrollments in the most commonly taught languages in the US institutions of higher education in selected years	70
5.2	Enrollment in Arabic in higher education institutions in the US in selected years.	70
5.3	HLL of Arabic by group	76

Preface

This book is based on the experience of more than 20 years of Teaching Arabic as a Foreign Language (TAFL), both in the Arab World and in North America. TAFL, as a field, has seen a unique growth in number of learners, material, and instructors within the last two decades and continues to grow every day. There have been developments in pedagogical approaches and curricula, including new, refined criteria to consider when defining learners of a foreign language. There is a need to give more attention to the increase in the number of Heritage Language Learners (HLLs). In the case of Arabic, there are the political, economic, and religious reasons for learning the Arabic language. The Arab World has been the center of economic resources and wealth, as well as global conflicts. All of this appears to have created a demand for learning Arabic, including both non-HLL and HLL. Little attention has been given to the HLL of Arabic. The increased interest in learning the language corresponds with an increase in the number of courses and programs offered at different levels of education. This also means that there is a larger number of instructors of Arabic, and with the growth in the number of instructors comes the need to share and exchange information. This is one of the main aims of this book.

Acknowledgments

Special thanks go to my family, you supported and encouraged me all the way; I am eternally grateful. Thank you to my colleagues and my students for the insightful discussions and for sharing their experiences.

List of abbreviations in alphabetical order

ABA	American-Born African
ACTFL	American Council of Teaching Foreign Languages
ALL	Arabic Language Learner
AUB	American University in Beirut
AUC	American University in Cairo
CA	Classical Arabic
CASA	Centre for Arabic Studies Abroad
CASLT	Canadian Association of Second Language Teachers
CEFR	Common European Framework of Reference for Languages
FLAP	Foreign Language Assistance Program
FSI	Foreign Service Institute
G-HLL	Geographic Heritage Language Learner
HL	Heritage Language
HLL	Heritage Language Learner
ILR	Interagency Language Roundtable
IELTS	International English Language Testing System
IM	Immigrant Minority
L1	First Language
L2	Second Language
LLS	Language Learning Strategies
MECAS	Middle East Centre for Arab Studies
MENA	Middle East and North Africa
M-HLL	Muslim Heritage Language Learner
MLA	Modern Languages Association
MSA	Modern Standard Arabic
NSLI	National Security Language Initiative
OPI	Oral Proficiency Interview
RM	Regional Minority
SLA	Second Language Acquisition
TAFL	Teaching Arabic as a Foreign Language
TOEFL	Test of English as a Foreign Language

Introduction

This book aims to fill a gap in available books in the field regarding Arabic and the HLL. To this day, HLLs' specific characteristics are rarely taken into account in either language classrooms or in language program design. The experiences and needs of HLLs in study abroad are a new and unexplored field, and one that could benefit the field of Arabic teaching. As it is a new sub-field in Second Language Acquisition (SLA), there has been a growing interest in studying it, but not enough work has been done regarding Arabic as an HLL. A look at research and studies related to HLLs of Arabic reveals the scarcity of work related to Arabic as a Heritage Language (HL). For instance, the *Heritage Language Journal* has been published since 2003, and up until 2019 there have been no papers published regarding Arabic as an HL. There is one review of a documentary about Arab HLLs in schools in the US. It is the belief of the author that the next few years will show a change in this regard as there has been a growing interest in Arabic as a foreign language in general, and eventually this will lead to the awareness of a gap to be filled regarding the unique group of learners: the HLLs of Arabic.

This book brings to light the current situation of TAFL in general and specifically presents an overall view of the HLL of Arabic. It is an addition to the work done in the field of SLA, as it is the first work of its kind in the field, focusing on HLLs and Arabic as a foreign language. This book is meant as a companion for Arabic language instructors and applied linguists interested in SLA.

The book is divided into two parts, and each part has three chapters. Chapter 1 starts by describing what is meant by a HL and how a HL is part of a heritage culture. It looks at groups of heritage language speakers in North America and in Europe in order to see how the same concept can be seen differently depending where you are in the world. Chapters 2 and 3 look at the Arabic language, both inside and outside the Arab World. Chapter 2 presents the key information about the Arabic language; it aims to answer questions about the Arabic language that a language learner might have or even find interesting to know. It starts by discussing Semitic languages and the main characteristics that distinguish Arabic from other languages. It also looks at the Arabic language today, what varieties of it there are, and how these varieties differ. It explains diglossia and how significant it is. Then, the chapter moves on to present the different sociolinguistic levels of Arabic, and continues by presenting the minority languages across the Arab

World in order to give a picture of the extent of the variety in language use in the Arab World. Next, Chapter 3 looks at Arabic in different communities. It also looks at the overlap between the Muslim World and the Arab World. The chapter illustrates how Arabic, even though it may not be the mother tongue used by the family, is nevertheless a cultural heritage. The last part of the chapter looks at Arabic and politics and how the general public in different parts of the world looks at the Arabic language.

The second part of the book focuses on the learners of Arabic, especially the HLL; it follows a practical approach built on the experience of professors in the field of teaching Arabic. It covers language pedagogy, the classroom, the curricula, and the educator. Chapter 4 is about the assessment of the HLL. The aim of the chapter is to point out the criteria of assessment that Arabic is measured against in order to ensure that the Arabic courses are working toward achieving these requirements. It presents the standard general methods of measuring proficiency and evaluating language levels that are widely recognized. It reviews both ACTFL in North America and CEFR in Europe, as well as other less popular proficiency guidelines and tests. If learners are expected to reach a certain proficiency level, then these levels have to not only be established, but also be clearly described and related to HLLs. Chapter 5 takes a close look at HLLs living in the West, both of Arabic and Muslim backgrounds. It presents a new approach to dividing the learners into two groups, explaining their differences and similarities. Finally, Chapter 6 looks at teaching Arabic as a HL. It looks at the Arabic classroom, reviews what has been written about Arabic as a HL, and includes examples of courses that have been developed or adapted for HLLs. The chapter looks at undergraduate university courses from North America and the UK to present the current situation in TAFL classrooms. The last section of the chapter looks at immersion programs, both in the US and in the Arab World to see how these programs work and how HLLs are placed in them.

One of the main aims of the book is to be a reference for those coming into the field of teaching Arabic, as well as being a resource for teachers of foreign languages. Based on that, it was decided that Arabic script would be avoided and that no special transliterations would be used. A second point to note is that the book is built on practical experience and wants to convey this. As the book looks mainly at university HLLs, not schoolchildren, the term professor is used to reflect the terminology used in higher education. The book explores a number of studies from the field, but there is still much research needed. Topics are discussed and analyzed based not only on research, but also on the experience of the author and colleagues. This book is based on a teacher's philosophy that every student's needs are of concern to educators, Arabic HLLs are important, and educators are capable of addressing the needs of Arabic HLLs, and so, improving their programs. Hopefully, the future will include more studies in these areas and more data will be available for further explorations.

Readership

Regarding audiences, Part 1 is meant to appeal to a much wider audience than simply Arabic teachers. It is of use to educators in the fields of language and society who are interested in Arabic – including diaspora and immigration studies, American studies, sociology, anthropology, and many others. Part 2 is helpful to all teachers of Arabic, as well as administrators who oversee language programs and departments. The teaching ideas are applicable across any language. This book is of interest wherever there are Arabic programs and HLLs: Europe and the UK, the Americas, or the MENA region. In the Arab World, this book would be particularly helpful for directors and instructors of Arabic in study abroad programs or other language centers.

For the experienced language instructor, the book brings together the reflections and interpretations of the current status of TAFL, as well as establishes the common criteria and features that have not been presented in a text before. This will serve as a reference for all those working in the field of TAFL and the field of SLA. As for students, this book is to be used as a resource by graduate students in the fields of linguistics, Arabic studies, and Middle East studies, as well as the social sciences generally. It is also of benefit to students who teach or anticipate teaching Arabic. Finally, the book is of interest to students involved in research in fields related to the role of Arabic in diverse societies – including social work, American studies, anthropology, sociology, urban studies, religion, and more.

Part 1
Arabic as a heritage language

Part 1 presents an overall look at heritage languages and the Arabic language. Chapter 1 starts by defining what is meant by a heritage language in general. Examples of heritage languages in the US, Canada, and Europe are outlined. This is followed, in Chapter 2, by a look at the Arabic language across the Arab World. Arabic diglossia is explained, and the varieties of Arabic are introduced. Then, in Chapter 3, Arabic outside the Arab world is looked at. The relation between Arabic and religion as well as the historic spread of Arabic are presented. Part 1 is meant as a general overview of the main issues the book covers: heritage language and Arabic. In order to do that, it starts by establishing the domains these cover so that in Part 2 the heritage language learner (HLL) of the Arabic classroom is presented in detail.

1 What is a heritage language?

1.0 Introduction

This book looks at what is meant by a heritage language (HL), who is a heritage language learner (HLL), and what needs to be known about this learner. It also looks at the Arabic language as a language used both inside and outside of the Arab World, as well as Arabic as a HL. HL learning is an emerging branch of linguistics, more specifically of Second Language Acquisition (SLA); more and more learners in the Arabic language class belong to this group. Over the last two decades, heritage language learning is becoming a recognized subbranch in second language learning. It is receiving attention in different places in both North America and Europe. Research in HL in both North America and Europe is growing for almost similar reasons. Chapter 1 looks at what is meant by a HL and how the term can vary in scope and meaning. The differences are a result of which language is discussed, where the language is used, and who is defining it. It also presents different groups of HLLs in different places in the West. The chapter aims at identifying the scope of this subfield in language learning, as well as sharing the progress in the field in order to better understand the language learners. This allows the reader to better place Arabic as a HL in context.

1.1 A definition of heritage language

As the name implies, a heritage language is a language of a people that belongs to the past: the near or far past. It can be the language of the parents, grandparents, or of an older people. This language is no longer the present dominant language at the place where the individual, in this case the HLL, lives. There are two main reasons why this language of the past is no longer present. It can be either because a group of speakers of this language moved away from the main group of speakers of the language; or it can be because a new group of people with a different language took over and became the dominant speakers in a place. Montrul (2010, p. 4) gives a broad definition of heritage speakers to be "child and adult members of a linguistic minority who grew up exposed to their home language and the majority language." Montrul looks at the HL development more as a form of bilingualism and does not discuss the linguistic proficiency nor the psychological, sociopolitical, or socioeconomic perspectives of HLs.

When discussing HLs, there are different distinctions that need to be clarified. In order to define what exactly is meant by an HL, one has to look at the location and the users of the language. Also, an attempt to explain how languages move from place to place clarifies how they become what is known as a HL. HL acquisition is developing in the US, Canada, and Europe. Even though the concept of HL is the same in all these places, it can be referred to in different terms, and its scope can vary according to the situation in the specific place where the HL is being used. There are external factors, both geographical and political, that affect the definition of HL. It is important to note that when this book discusses HL, it is limiting it to HL in the field of language learning and from the foreign language educator's point of view. The book does not look at the cultural, social, or anthropological perspectives, as these would be different.

This chapter looks at HLs in the US and Canada (North America[1]) and how they differ and change. Also, it briefly looks at HLs in Europe, as this shows the reader how the concept of HLs differs with place.[2] The chapter looks at language policy and how HL education is not the same in all places and how it is influenced by elements such as history, politics, and demographics. The last section in this chapter gives a brief outline of a number of HLs in North America. This establishes the ground to see how Arabic as a HL fits in the bigger scope of HLs.

A definition of all that is incorporated in the term "heritage language learner" is more than often incomplete, as this changes from place to place, from time to time, and from language to language, as well as differing according to the approach to the topic. The following section looks at a number of different types of HLs in order to present a clear idea of what is meant by the term. HLs differ from one place to another according to where the HL is; they are influenced by elements such as history, politics, and demographics. For the average North American, when we talk about HL, the first thing that comes to mind is the language spoken and used by Native Americans, the indigenous people, who inhabited North America before the Europeans ever arrived to this land. This is partly true, but, as we have seen above, HL has grown in the world of today to include much more than the language of the indigenous people.

With the continuous flow of immigrants into North America, there has been a continuous growth in the number of languages these people bring with them, especially after the political changes the world saw during the twentieth century and continue to see until the present time. Thus, a general definition of the HL in the field of language learning is, as Fishman (2001) explains, the language that students are exposed to at home. It occurs in the case where the family speaks another language at home and does not speak the main language of the community. This learner is familiar, to a certain extent, with the home language, but is not necessarily proficient in it. They can be developed in the speaking and listening skills more than the written skills as they might not have been formally taught to read and write this language (see Section 5.2).

Heritage languages are usually languages of the past; they belong to the family history – the connection to the past can be gone or it can still be present. The reason why they are of the past can differ. One way to divide or group HLs is based on when in the past were they used and why they ceased to become the language of the majority. Fishman (2001) and Makoni (2018) talk about different types of HLs, and they discuss definitions given by other linguists. HLs can be classified in different ways, and a brief summary of how both linguists see HL is presented below. They look at languages based on the time these languages were used in North America and follow a chronological order starting with the oldest languages used followed by the more recent ones.

Fishman (2001) classifies three categories of heritage languages: indigenous heritage languages, colonial heritage languages, and immigrant heritage languages; a fourth category or group of HL is ancestral heritage languages, which is discussed by Makoni (2018). These groups are briefly presented below.

1.1.1 Indigenous heritage languages

Indigenous heritage languages are the languages that were spoken in the US and Canada before English, Spanish, or French was ever spoken on the continent. The exact number of the languages spoken in the US and Canada before the first settlers arrived is estimated to be between 300 languages (Krauss, 1998) and 450 (Burnaby, 2007); it is difficult to know the exact number. Today there are around 155 indigenous languages in use to various degrees, with 57 of these languages spoken by a few elderly people only and not by the younger population. These languages were not accepted the Europeans. Early after arriving in North America, they worked on establishing the European languages on the new continent and minimized the presence of indigenous languages.

In the nineteenth century, Residential Schools were established in the US and in Canada. The main aim of the schools was to assimilate the indigenous children into the European ways of life including language, culture, and Christianity (Smith, 2010). The experience of the indigenous students in the residential boarding schools was extremely negative. In Canada, from the 1870s until the mid-1990s, when the last school was closed, more than 150,000 indigenous students were sent to Residential Schools where they were forced to forget not only their language, but also their culture and traditions (Wilk, Maltby, & Cook, 2017). The position of the governments of the US and Canada has changed over time. The former Canadian Prime Minister, Stephen Harper, has apologized for the Indian Residential School System (Government of Canada, 2008). Today, the number of speakers and users of the indigenous heritage languages is decreasing and the government has acknowledged the gravity of the system that tried to eradicate the identity of the first inhabitants of North America, and it has established a system where the language and culture are being supported and encouraged. Teaching indigenous languages is supported by the government, and university programs in Indigenous Studies are welcomed.

1.1.2 Colonial heritage languages

Colonial heritage languages refer to the languages that were spoken mainly in the US by the settlers who arrived before the English speakers. This includes Spanish, Dutch, French, and German. These languages were part of the earlier languages used in the US, but as the majority of new immigrants at the time were from Britain, English became the language of the majority. German was the only language that continued to be the mother tongue of speakers across the generations, is still used in parts of Pennsylvania. This is for reasons specific to this particular group of speakers, who held on to the language as part of their culture and identity. Yet, at times German was looked upon with suspicion in the US (see Section 1.2).

It can be argued that even the English language came to the US with the immigrants, so it was a colonial language, not a HL; it has become the official language of the country and as such it is no longer neither a colonial language nor a HL.

1.1.3 Immigrant heritage languages

Immigrant heritage languages is a term used to refer to languages that came with immigrants from their motherlands after the US became an independent country. These include Spanish, German, and Italian, among other languages. Often these languages will overlap with the colonial language, such as in the case of Spanish. Actually, Spanish is the most prominent case of modern HLs in the US, and the research on Spanish as a HL is key to this emerging field.

Immigrant HLs in the US can be divided the into three stages based on the chronological facts and the role of political events on HLs. This immigrant HL group saw changes at three key turning-points: (a) after independence, (b) after World War II, and (c) the turn of the century, more specifically after 2011. These crucial turning points in the history of the US have led to a change in the public views and attitudes to certain HLs. For instance, Fishman (2001) points out that the view of the immigrant languages changed considerably during WWII. Not all languages were treated equally. If one looks at the case of German, for example, one will notice that the German speakers were eyed with suspicion and there was a decline in the registration in the schools teaching German at that time.

1.1.4 Ancestral heritage languages

Makoni (2018) notes that the languages of the African Americans is a distinct group of its own, which he refers to as the ancestral heritage languages. Makoni (2018) explains that the HL(s) of the American-born Africans (ABAs) has been lost, as it was spoken generations back and the users stopped speaking it. Generations later, there is interest in learning these languages again. There is a current wave of revival, learning the languages of the grandparents and great-grandparents from the land far away. This HL was gone, but it represents an identity; as a matter of fact, the American universities have seen an increase in the number of learners of the ancestral HL. Makoni (2018) presents a case worth noting, which is the recent growth of interest in HL(s) of ABAs in the US. His study looks at third generation ABAs and how they learn the HL to maintain an identity and to have a link with where they came from, even if it is a faraway land that they never visit. Similar to the indigenous HL, it represents part of the heritage of the learner who comes back to it after three generations. Unlike the indigenous HL, the HL of the ABAs was never the language of the place where they lived, for it is far and distant, but as this type of HL is neither immigrant nor indigenous, it can be referred to it as the ancestral HL (see Section 1.2.2).

1.1.5 Minority languages – Canada

In Canada, in modern times, there has been a general commitment for language education for languages other than English, mainly because Canada has English and French as two official languages. Canada protects both official languages, as well as the teaching of the other non-official languages that Canadians more than often want to learn. Duff & Li (2009) point out that Canada has been a pioneer when it comes to HL research, largely because of the French–English duality that exists in the country. Minority language learning is the right given to Francophones to learn French outside French-speaking areas or the right of Anglophones to learn English in the French-speaking province of Quebec. It also ensures that all Canadians have access to learn both official languages of Canada (Duff & Li, 2009). In Canada, HL education is the term used to refer to learning languages that are neither official nor indigenous but are related to the learners through the family and cultural background.

1.2 Heritage languages and language policy in the United States

Language learning policy plays an important role in the development of language learning programs, and the US is no exception to that. There is no official language policy in the US and each state is left to formulate the language policies it sees as most appropriate. Thus, as is noted by the Center of Applied Linguistics (2018), all states have English as one of their official languages. A number of states have more than one official language, for example New Mexico and the Commonwealth of Puerto Rico both have English and Spanish as two official languages, and Hawaii has both English and Hawaiian as the two official languages of the state. The general trend in the US has been the development of English. At points this was stressed, and the Anglo culture was imposed on minorities. This has been the case with the deculturation of American Indians. The Residential Schools that were established from the early nineteenth century until the mid-twentieth century reflect the European approach towards the indigenous population. The US policy changed on this matter with the Native American Languages Act of 1990, which recognizes and supports the indigenous languages and gives the natives the right to use their own languages (Krauss, 1998). This might be too little too late as the decline in the use of indigenous HLs continues and the heritage speakers seem to prefer using the English language.

Another example is the case of German in the United States. Again, with no official language policy, German speakers were forced to use English-only during and after World War I in order to avoid the persecution and the backlash that they would face if they were seen as German, not Anglo-American. This affected the use of German among the immigrants from German-speaking countries, to the extent that the German newspapers were almost stopped, and people changed their German names to more American ones; German was seen as the language of the enemy. German became used mainly among the Mennonite communities in the Midwest. Mennonites arrived around 1865 to Kansas, and used German, their first language, at home, and in church, and they did not get involved in politics. Yet, in 1917, they were regarded as siding with the enemy even though most of them were either naturalized Americans or were born in America (Capozzola, 2008).

The general, non-written policy throughout most of the twentieth century was to support and build the Anglo culture as part of the American identity; yet, a change has been seen from the end of the century to the present time. In 1988, the Foreign Language Assistance Program (FLAP) was established. It is the only federally funded program that exclusively targets foreign language instruction to elementary and secondary schools. A decade later, that program was refocused to give priority to the instruction in what was referred to as critical foreign languages – Arabic, Chinese, Japanese, Korean, Russian, and languages in the Indic, Iranian, and Turkic families (US Department of Education, 2008). In 2006, President Bush announced the establishment of the National Security Language Initiative (NSLI), aiming to increase the number of US residents learning, speaking, and teaching critically needed foreign languages. The NSLI gives opportunities to students at schools, teachers, and university undergraduate and graduate students to study critical languages in the US and abroad. It is a national plan developed by the US Departments of Education, State, Defense, and the Office of the Director of National Intelligence. Each department has developed a number of programs and offered scholarships to encourage students to learn the critical languages at different levels of education – from primary school to university (both undergraduate and graduate) – as well as language teachers.

The growth of interest in learning the critical languages has also meant that many second and third generation Americans from families that speak, or spoke, one of the languages offered registered to learn their own heritage language – which also happens to be a critical language according to the NSLI. It is important to note that these programs are open to all students, heritage and non-heritage learners; whereas the first group saw it as connecting with their family roots, the second group saw it as a chance to learn about the world outside of America. Many of the university undergraduate students who were awarded these scholarships are now perusing a career in teaching these critical languages (see Chapter 6.1).

1.2.1 Heritage languages in the United States – Spanish

There are more than 350 languages spoken across the US (United States Census Bureau, 2015); immigrant HLs constitute a large number of these languages. The HLs in the US vary in the number of their speakers and how they are regarded in the US. The Spanish heritage speakers form the largest HL group in the US – followed by Chinese speakers. There are a few states where Spanish is not the largest HL; in these exceptional states, other HLs come first. For instance, French is the largest HL in Louisiana, Maine, New Hampshire, and Vermont; German in North Dakota; and Filipino/Tagalog and Japanese are the number one HLs in Hawaii (Nagano, 2015). Spanish arrived to the US in 1513, when the explorer Juan Ponce de León came ashore in present-day Florida. It has been present ever since, with an increasing number of speakers. The longstanding presence has led to different dialects of Spanish used across the US. Today, the Spanish HL speakers come from different backgrounds and they are not all one group; they are not all from Spain. In fact, the number of Spanish speakers from Spain has declined and more and more Spanish-speaking Latin-American groups of speakers are present. Not all Spanish speakers belong to one group: there are Caribbean dialects; Spanish from places such as Puerto Rico, Cuba, and Dominican Republic; as well as inland Spanish dialects from Chile, Argentina, Colombia, and Mexico.

An important point to notice is that Spanish as a HL is maintained by the speakers. They do not stop using the language in the home or even outside, while other HL speakers stop using the HL. The HL speakers of Spanish are proficient in the language and they do no stop passing the language to the following generation once they come to the US. There is more than one possible reason for this. First, Spanish is typologically not far from English – it is closer to English than Chinese is, for example. Second, the Spanish language has been present in the US for a very long time; it is not a recent HL, such as Arabic is for example.

1.2.2 Heritage languages in the United States – American-born Africans

When discussing HLs, each language and group of people is discussed separately, such as Spanish, French, and Arabic. This might not be always accurate; the American-born Africans are a case in point. For this group of learners, we can group them as one group, since the grandchildren are of African descent born in the US who can trace their origins to Africa – in some cases their families can come from more than one place – and their ancestral language(s) all belong to Africa. It is as if Africa is one homeland and the African identity is grouped as one; even though this is not completely accurate, African Americans are often seen as one group. The main focus here is on the languages they learn, not on the political grouping of American-born Africans. The interest in learning languages used by grandparents three or more generations ago is what is of interest here. Makoni (2018) looks at the language(s) used by their grandparents and how they were prohibited for economic, social, and political reasons from using this language, leading the second generation to use it less and less. The third generation, according to Makoni (2018), has lost their grandparents' language and use English; but this generation has developed an interest in connecting with their roots, with the language of a place that they've heard of and feel they belong to. They seem to want to learn their ancestral language as a way of maintaining, or finding, their identity.

Makoni (2018) collects his qualitative data from in-depth interviews with ABAs to come up with the conclusion that the HL is part of the heritage identity. Even when the first two generations have ignored the HL and allowed it to fade until it almost disappeared, the third generation is coming back to the HL. This is not only to maintain an identity, but they can even make use of it in our modern world today for their economic benefit. Even though the HL of ABAs is not the most widely spread HL in the US, it has a number of characteristics that link it to HL of American-born Arabs (see Section 1.3.1).

1.3 Heritage languages and language policy in Canada

Canada is officially a bilingual country, with English and French both being official languages. Canada has been working on developing language policies to ensure that both English- and French-speaking Canadians have access to all services in the official language they prefer. It recognizes minority, indigenous, and immigrant languages. Thus, in Canada the language education context has three groups of languages to consider: the indigenous language, the minority language, and the heritage language.

Canada, on the social level, is highly multilingual, with so many speakers using a third language in their day-to-day life. These multilingual speakers are heritage speakers, either of languages from immigrant countries that their parents or grandparents came from or they are speakers of indigenous languages native to Canada long before the British and French settled in Canada. Duff and Li (2009) report that approximately 20 percent of Canadians reported in the last Canadian census that they speak a non-official language at home. The rights of the indigenous population were not always granted (as was the case in the US), but in 2019 the Indigenous Languages Act (Statutes of Canada 2019. Chapter 23.) was issued and is a step toward recognizing the significance and importance of indigenous heritage languages and supporting their revitalization.

Canada, being officially a bilingual country, has had language policies and acts drawn and revised more than once. The main focus is on the state of the two official languages. For instance, the Official Language Policies of the Canadian Provinces looks at the language policy regarding the difference between the two official languages and how the minority language in each province is managed (Vaillancourt, Coche, Cadieux, & Ronson, 2012). It looks at each province and the facilities and costs it provides for each of the two languages in relation to the speakers in this province, but it does not consider HLs. This is because while the federal policy makers focus on the official languages, the HLs are dealt with on the provincial level; the provinces look at HLs, each province on its own terms. The right given to each Canadian to learn both official languages is maintained in most of the provinces. The province that stands out as different in its support to official languages is Quebec, where the province is officially French. The provincial government supports the French language since there is a deep concern that English, as a majority language across Canada, can take over Quebec as well. This is why the provincial laws emphasize French over English. Immigrant HLs are taught across the province, at weekend schools, or at private schools, as well as at the universities even when one official language is placed ahead of the other in the provincial language policy.

As for indigenous language education given to the original inhabitants of Canada, the policy has changed over time. Indigenous communities in Canada had 450 spoken languages, from 11 language families, around the year 1500. The Canadian government's policies on indigenous education in the past forced the natives to speak English or French, which led to a dramatic decrease in the number of speakers of these languages. When parents stop talking the HL, the language of their ancestors, with their children, then the language goes away. The intergenerational transmission of the language is necessary to ensure the continuity and presence of a HL (Extra & Gorter, 2001). The loss as a result of a language policy taking away a HL from a minority group is difficult to reverse, but not impossible.

There are recent attempts to amend the formal language policies. The federal government has come to recognize the importance of revitalization and maintenance of these languages and is currently working on supporting this process by developing new language programs across the education system. The Indigenous Languages Act is an important step in that direction. An example of the progress made on this level is the fact that in 1999, Nunavut declared Inuktitut, Inuinnaqtun, French, and English as its official languages.

Language policies in Canada officially support HLs of immigrants and policies. In 1977, the Canadian federal government created a cultural enrichment program and one of its roles was to support the teaching of non-official languages (Burnaby, 2007). This meant mainly the immigrant languages, while the native indigenous languages, for political reasons, were treated separately. Federal policies are not always immediately reflected in practical steps. Schools resisted teaching HLs and also, they were not given fiscal support. At the moment, the support for immigrant HLs differs from one province to another.

1.3.1 Heritage languages in the United States and Canada – Arabic

The number of US native speakers of Arabic is increasing. According to the Center for Immigration Studies, Arabic is one of the top languages that has seen an increase in the number of speakers in the US; it has 1.2 million speakers in the US which puts it in the fifth place, along with French, spoken in the US after Spanish, Chinese, Tagalog and Vietnamese (Zeigler & Camarota, 2018). Burton looks at the top languages used in the US, and the number of those who report using Arabic at home is 924,374, which makes Arabic one of the top ten languages used in the US (number nine) (Burton, 2018).

Arabic is a HL that does not belong to one country, but to a larger geographical area. It is one language spoken across the Arab World in Africa and Asia.

American-born Arabs all come from the Arab World; they can come from more than 20 Arabic speaking countries. Arabic HL speakers, similar to ABA HL speakers mentioned earlier, come from a large geographic area. Heritage speakers in both groups do not come from one ethnic background – ABAs come from different sub-Saharan countries or tribes that are distinct and American-born Arabs are also not one homogenous ethnic group. Arabs include those from Assyrian, Nomadic, Pharaonic, Phoenician, Tuareg, and other ethnic origins, but they all share one language, as well as other common qualities.

As Arabs do not all come from one country, with time, you can find a family of American-born Arabs in which the grandparents come from two or three different countries (same as in the case of ABAs). Another common point shared between these two groups is that both the American-born Africans and American-born Arabs are visible minorities. Their heritage culture is very often seen in their dress code, their food, and many other day-to-day matters more than the case of the American culture, which is largely European based, that forms the majority

Due to the diglossia, and the existence of at least two varieties of Arabic in every Arab country (see Section 2.2), this results in the presence of a number of spoken dialects that the language user would recognize as his HL. Modern Standard Arabic (MSA) is the one written variety that they all share, and they can as well use the spoken MSA variety to speak to each other across the 22 Arab countries. Often the HLL feels confused about the variety they have to learn; it is as if they have to learn two different varieties when they learn Arabic. The case of HLLs of Arabic is looked at closely in Chapter 5.

1.4 Heritage languages in Europe

A point to note is that there is a difference between HLs in North America and HLs in Europe due to the difference in history, languages, and demographics between Europe and North America. North America has been open to immigration and new immigrants as they were needed to build the growing countries, while Europe was already established. It was the Europeans who first went over to North America to find a future in the new colonies of the time; the new settlers moved across the ocean for a better future. In other words, Europeans moved across the Atlantic Ocean and took their immigrant languages with them. Today, the immigration still continues, but at much lower rates.

In our present day, the difference between Europe and North America in how HLs are seen is reflected in the choice of terms used to describe the concept of HLs, which is present in both North America and Europe. In North America the term *heritage languages* refers to the languages used by immigrants or indigenous people. As De Bot and Gorter (2005) point out, in Europe the term *minority language* is more commonly used to refer to the languages of groups of immigrants. The division of the minority language is into two groups: regional minority (RM) languages and immigrant minority (IM) languages. These terms were used by Extra and Gorter (2001) and have since been widely accepted in the field of applied linguistics. Thus, the three categories of heritage language that Fishman

(2001) talks about when discussing the US become two types of *minority* languages in Europe:

1. Regional minority languages have been present in Europe for a long time and the speakers are European, not immigrants. The RM languages include Welsh, Catalan, and Basque. The maintenance of RM languages is supported by the European Union. The Eurobarometer 386 report (European Commission, 2012) uses *regional indigenous language*, with an interesting definition of "indigenous" that differs from how it is used in the North American context.
2. Immigrant minority languages came to Europe with migrant workers or migrants from former colonies. The first group includes Moroccans moving to France or the Turks moving to Germany. The former colonies' migrants include the Algerians in France, Pakistani and Indian in the United Kingdom, or immigrants from Surinam moving to the Netherlands. These languages are also referred to as *non-indigenous regional languages* by the European Union in the Eurobarometer 386 report (European Commission, 2012).

Extra and Gorter (2001) talk about the official state languages, RM languages, and the IM languages. They note that RM and IM languages have common points, but they also differ from one another. Language policies towards RM and IM languages also differ by the fact that RM languages have been taught at some schools going back to the nineteenth century.

One of the main language differences between North America and Europe is in the number of languages used in each location. North America is predominantly monolingual, except for Mexico and Quebec. In the US and Canada, English is the language everybody uses outside of the house as it is the official language of communication, with the exception of Quebec where French is the language used – together with English – at times. The case of Europe is very different; Europe is multilingual, with a diversity of languages equal to, and even higher than, the number of states in the continent. In Europe different languages exist across relatively smaller geographical areas. Europe has 23 official languages and more than 60 RM and IM languages, according to the survey conducted by the European Union in 2012 (European Commission, 2012). The proximity of different language speakers to one another in relatively smaller areas creates an awareness to bilingualism and multilingualism. North America is made up of immigrants who came across in different waves over time; this has led to a different view on language since English is the only official language in the US, English and French in Canada, and Spanish in Mexico. Thus the 23 official languages in Europe are down to only three in North America, with English being by far the language with the highest number of speakers.

There has been a noticeable increase in the number of immigrants to Europe and North America. Many of these immigrants are not from the West and they bring with them non-Western languages such as Arabic, Chinese, Hindi, Persian, and others. This has led to an increase in the number of immigrant/minority languages as well as an increase in the variety of languages and language families that the immigrant languages bring with them to their new communities. The HL has HL speakers, yet after a while the speakers might not use the HL as often as the first generation. Eventually, with the second or third generation, there is a point where the HL is not fully acquired by the younger generation, and this is when the HLL realizes that they need to formally learn the language of their family in order to reach the proficiency level they desire.

Notes

1 The book looks at the state of heritage languages in the United States and Canada when it refers to North America unless otherwise mentioned.
2 A complete discussion of HLs in Europe is beyond the scope of this book. There is a difference in languages and history that makes HLs differ in certain aspects between Europe than North America.

Bibliography

Burnaby, B. (2008). Language policy and education in Canada, volume 1: Language policy and political issues in education. In N.H. Hornberger (Ed.), *Encyclopedia of language and education*. Boston, MA: Springer

Burton, J. (2018, June). *The most spoken languages in America*. Retrieved June 2019, from https://www.worldatlas.com/articles/the-most-spoken-languages-in-america.html.

Capozzola, C. (2008). *Uncle Sam wants you: World War I and the making of the modern American citizen*. New York: Oxford University Press.

Center for Applied Linguistics. (2018). US educational policy. Retrieved June 3, 2018, from http://www.cal.org/areas-of-impact/language-planning-policy/US-educational-language-policy.

De Bot, K., & Gorter, D. (2005). A European perspective on heritage languages in the modern language journal. *The Modern Language Journal*, *89*(4 (Winter)), 612–616. Published by: Wiley on behalf of the National Federation of Modern Language Teachers Associations Stable URL. Retrieved May 14, 2018, from http://www.jstor.org/stable/3588634.

Duff, P. A., & Li, D. (2009). Indigenous, minority, and heritage language education in Canada: Policies, contexts, and issues. *The Canadian Modern Language Review/La Revue canadienne des langues vivantes*, *66*(1), 1–8. doi: 10.3138/cmlr.66.1.001.

European Commission. (2012). *Special Eurobarometer 386 Europeans and their languages*. European Commission, Conducted by TNS Opinion & Social at the request of Directorate-General Education and Culture, Directorate-General for Translation and Directorate-General for Interpretation.

Extra, G., & Gorter, D. (2001). *The other languages of Europe demographic, sociolinguistic and educational perspectives*. UK: Multilingual Matters. Clevedon: Cromwell Press Ltd.

Fishman, J. (2001). 300-Plus years of heritage language education in the United States. In J. K. Peyton, D. A. Ranard, & S. McGinnis (Ed.), *Heritage languages in America: Preserving a national resource* (pp. 81–89). Washington, DC & McHenry, IL: Center for Applied Linguistics & Delta Systems.

Government of Canada. (2008, June 11). *Statement of apology – to former students of Indian Residential Schools*. Retrieved from Indigenous and Northern Affairs Canada https://www.aadnc-aandc.gc.ca/eng/1100100015644/1100100015649.

Kelleher, A. (2018, May 22). *Who is a heritage language learner?* Retrieved from Heritage Briefs Heritage Briefs http://www.cal.org/heritage/.

Krauss, M. (1998). The condition of Native North American languages: The need for realistic assessment and action. *International Journal of the Sociology of Language*, *132*(1), 9–21.

Makoni, B. (2018). Beyond country of birth: Heritage language learning and the discursive construction of identities of resistance. *Heritage Language Journal*, *15*(1), 71–94.

Montrul, S. (2010). Current issues in heritage language acquisition. *Annual Review of Applied Linguistics*, *30*, 3–23. doi:10.1017/S0267190510000103.

Nagano, T. (2015). Demographics of adult heritage language speakers in the United States: Differences by region and language and their implications. *Modern Language Journal*, *99*(4), 771–792.

Smith, A. (2010, April). *Indigenous peoples and boarding schools: A comparative study*. Retrieved from United Nations Economic and Social Council https://webcache.goo gleusercontent.com/search?q=cache:XO9mYRCwxTcJ:https://www.un.org/esa/socde v/unpfii/documents/E%2520C.19%25202010%252011.DOC+&cd=10&hl=en&ct =clnk&gl=kw&client=safari.

Statutes of Canada 2019 Chapter 23. (2019, June 21). *Bill C-91 An Act respecting Indigenous languages*. Retrieved October 2019, from https://www.parl.ca/DocumentViewer/ en/42-1/bill/C-91/royal-assent

United States Census Bureau. (2015, November 2015). *United States census report 2015*. Retrieved December 2018, from United States Census Bureau: https://www.census. gov/newsroom/press-releases/2015/cb15-185.html

U.S. Department of Education. (2008). *Enhancing foreign language proficiency in the United States: Preliminary results of the National Security Language Initiative*. Washington, D.C.: Office of Postsecondary Education.

Vaillancourt, F., Coche, O., Cadieux, M. A., & Ronson, J. L. (2012). *Official language policies of the Canadian Provinces costs and benefits in 2006*. FraserInstitute / www. fraserinstitute.org

Wilk, P., Maltby, A., & Cook, M. (2017). Residential schools and the effects on Indigenous health and well-being in Canada—a scoping review. *Public Health Reviews*, *38*(8), doi:10.1186/s40985-017-0055-6.

Zeigler, K., & Camarota, S. A. (2018). *Almost half speak a foreign language in america's largest cities*. Washington, DC: Centre for Immigration Studies.

Additional References

Ajrouch, K., & Jamal, A. (2007). Assimilating to a white identity: The case of Arab Americans. *The International Migration Review*, *41*(4), 860–879.

Al-Hazza, Tami Craft, & Bucher, Katherine T. (2010). Bridging a cultural divide with literature about Arabs and Arab Americans. *Middle School Journal*, *41*(3), 4–11. JSTOR. Retrieved from www.jstor.org/stable/23047567.

Ball, J. (2009). Supporting young indigenous children's language development in Canada: A review of research on needs and promising practices, the Canadian modern language review. *The Canadian Modern Language Review/La Revue Canadienne des Langues Vivantes*, *66*(1), 19–47. doi:10.3138/cmlr.66.1.019.

Canadian Education Association. (1991). *Heritage language programs in Canadian school boards*. Toronto: Canadian Education Association.

Centre for Immigration Studies, Zeigler, K., & Camarota, S. A. (2018). *Almost half speak a foreign language in America's largest cities*. Retrieved June 18, 2019 from https://cis.org/sites/default/files/2018-09/zeigler-language-18_1.pdf

Cummins, J. (1992). Heritage language teaching in Canadian schools. *Journal of Curriculum Studies*, *24*(3), 287–296.

Driessen, G., van der Slik, F., & de Bot, K. (2002). Home language and language proficiency: A large-scale longitudinal study in Dutch primary schools. *Journal of Multilingual and Multicultural Development*, *23*(3), 175–194.

European Commission. (2012). Europeans and their languages report, special barometer 386. Retrieved from http://ec.europa.eu/commfrontoffice/publicopinion/archives/ebs/ebs_386_en.pdf

Higgins, C. (2019). Special issue: Language, heritage and family: A dynamic perspective. *International Journal of the Sociology of Language*, issue *255*.

Hinton, L. (1998). Language loss and revitalization in California: Overview. *International Journal of the Sociology of Language*, *132*(1), 83–93.

Hornberger, N. H., & Wang, S. C. (2008). Who are our heritage language learners? Identity and biliteracy in heritage language education in the United States. In D. Brinton, O. Kagan & S. Bauckus (Eds.), *Heritage language education. A new field emerging* (pp. 3–35). New York: Routledge.

Iverson, M. (2014). Spanish as a heritage language in the United States: The state of the field. *Journal of Spanish Language Teaching*, *1*(2), 228–229. doi:10.1080/23247797.2014.961369.

Kagan, O. (2008). *What is a heritage language?* Retrieved from http://www.international.ucla.edu/languages/news/article.asp?parentid=93215.

Polinsky, M., & Kagan, O. (2007). Heritage languages: In the 'wild' and in the classroom. *Language and Linguistics Compass*, *1/5*, 368–395. Journal Compilation Blackwell Publishing Ltd. doi: 10.1111/j.1749-818x.2007.00022.x.

Valdés, G. (2005). Bilingualism, heritage language learners, and SLA research: Opportunities lost or seized? *The Modern Language Journal*, *89*(3), 410–426.

Valdés, G. (2012). *Spanish as a heritage language in the United States: The state of the field* (Beaudrie S. & Fairclough M., Eds.). Georgetown University Press. Retrieved from www.jstor.org/stable/j.ctt2tt42d.

Wiley, T. G., & Valdes, G. (Eds.) (2000). Editors' introduction: Heritage language instruction in the United States: A time for renewal (Special Issue). *Bilingual Research Journal*, *24*(4) iii–vii

2 Arabic language(s) in the Arab World

2.0 Introduction

This chapter presents all the information necessary about the Arabic language that the language learner might need. The learner expects to learn basic information about the language such as where the language is spoken and what is the difference between the Arab World, the Muslim World, and the Middle East. What people know about the Arabic language differs from one person to another based on who the person is, where the person is from, and what they do, or intend to do, in life. The Arabic language for the Western world is different to the Arabic language to the Muslim World, for example. Also, what a language represents can depend on what one does in life. That is why Arabic for a politician is different to Arabic for a clergyman or a businessman. People see language from their own individual perspective, be that academic, social, religious, economic, or other. When they come to learn the language, they have questions about the language itself and they welcome the opportunity to learn about Arabic while learning the language itself. They expect the language professor to be able to share information about the language and answer these questions.

This chapter starts by presenting basic information about Arabic as a Semitic language and the main characteristics of the language, in order to be able to understand where the Arabic language comes from, how it is built, and how it works as a language. Then, it looks at the Arabic language today – what varieties of the language exist and how do these varieties differ. It also explains diglossia and how significant it is as a linguistic feature of Arabic. After that, the chapter moves on to the usage of the language and presents the different social "levels" of Arabic the native speakers use, from Classical Arabic (CA) to street-dialect as discussed by Badawi (Badawi, 1973). This information is often partially known to the learners, but it is important to ensure that the students have all the basic information they need to understand how the language works, not learning only the language in isolation from the social, non-linguistic information that could help learners understand the language and its speakers better and thus ultimately learn it better.

As part of providing the learner with a scope of the language, the chapter looks at minority languages in the Arab World. Learners are very often unaware of minority languages spoken in the Arab World, such as Kurdish in Northern Iraq,

Amazigh in North Africa, and many others. Most of the speakers of minority languages are bilingual and use Arabic outside the house, in public, day-to-day communications.

2.1 Arabic: A Semitic language

Language educators know from their personal experience that adult language learners almost always want to "learn about the language" and how it works; they want to know how similar or different it is to English and other languages they know. When adult learners come to learn a new language, they usually expect to know more about the language they are learning, such as the main characteristics of the language or key similarities to and main differences from their mother tongue, if any. The history of the language is not usually a top priority, but based on experience, students usually find it informative and appreciate knowing more information about the speakers and the culture of the language they are learning.

Arabic is a Semitic language; Semitic languages spread across North Africa and Southwest Asia. This family of languages has been present in the Middle East for thousands of years. Arabic belongs to a family of languages that is spoken by more than 500 million speakers. Today, according to the Arabic League report in 2017, Arabic is the most widely spoken Semitic language with more than 400 million native speakers across the Arab World (League of Arab States, 2017). Other Semitic languages spoken today include Amharic, Tigrigna, and Hebrew. The term *Semitic* was first used in the eighteenth century and the term is originally a biblical term – referring to Shem, the son of Abraham (Demeke, 2001). The Semitic language is one of the six Afroasiatic families. Arabic is one of the important Semitic languages with the largest number of users.

The Semitic languages differ from Germanic, Latin, or Slavic languages found across Europe in several ways. To start with, there is the script; all romance languages, as well as English, are written in the Latin alphabet – with modifications. The Arabic script is different and does not use the Latin alphabet but uses an Arabic alphabet or Arabic *abjad*. Also, Arabic is written from right to left and books open from the right, so one actually turns the pages opposite than is done with an English text. As a practical point for teaching, the first day of the Beginners Arabic class, the professor should explain to the learners that they have two options, either to start writing from the back of their notebooks or to turn the paper bottom up so that margins are on the right side and they can write the Arabic language on the correct side of the copy book. All students find differences between Arabic and other languages interesting and they want to learn more. In addition, with the writing system comes a lot of explaining about how the long vowels are part of the alphabet, but short vowels are *diacritics* that are written above the letters. Furthermore, the fact that Arabic does not have capital and small letters but has letters that change their shape depending on their position in a word is one of the first things learners find out about the language. Another difference that students note from the start between Semitic languages and English is in the phonology – the sounds of the language. There are sounds in Arabic that don't exist in English, just as there are English sounds absent in Arabic. This is one area where students come to learn more about their own language while learning Arabic.

Language learners at the university level are usually keen to know how the language works, for this reason it is useful to explain to them that Arabic is a derivational language where prefixes, infixes, and suffixes are used. It is also useful to introduce the root system in word formation at an early stage of learning the language; this helps learners build their vocabulary and have a better overall picture of how the language works on a morphological level. The fact that the words: to write, writer(s), book(s), office(s), desk(s), library(ies), letter(s), written, and correspondence all come from the same three consonant roots (k, t, b), which enables learners to visualize how they can group words and build vocabulary from an early stage once they understand how the root system and language patterns work.

2.2 Diglossia

It is agreed upon by the general public that Arabic is not an easy language to learn for English speakers. This perception of Arabic as difficult can intimidate language learners. One of the main reasons behind this assumption is diglossia; the existence of a written and spoken variety[1] of Arabic that are quite distinct from one another. Arabic has two different varieties, a formal Classical Arabic (CA) and an informal spoken variety. This characteristic linguistic variation in Arabic is one of the points that learners want to understand from the beginning even though it is not clear to the learner how exactly diglossia works. The learners cannot fully understand at the initial stages of learning the language how the two varieties work side by side. What is diglossia? Why are there two varieties? Should they learn the two varieties or just one? To answer these questions, we will briefly present the basic outline of how diglossia developed and what it entails.

The term was used for the first time by Charles Ferguson, an esteemed linguist who worked in the Middle East in the 1940s and 1950s and taught Arabic at Harvard in the 1950s until he resigned to establish the Center for Applied Linguistics.[2] In 1959, Charles Ferguson introduced the term *diglossia* for the first time in his article "Diglossia" (Ferguson, 1959a). He uses the term to describe the situation in which "two varieties of a language exist side by side throughout the community, with each having a definite role to play" (Ferguson, 1959a, p. 325). Diglossia is a feature of other languages, such as Modern Greek, Swiss German, and Haitian Creole; Arabic diglossia has been in use for the longest time. Ferguson defines diglossia as:

> a relatively stable language situation in which, in addition to the primary dialects of the language (which may include a standard or regional standards), there is a very divergent, highly codified (often grammatically more complex) super-imposed variety, the vehicle of a large and respected body of written literature, either in an earlier period or in another speech community, which is learned largely by formal education and is used for most written and

formal spoken purposes but is not used by any sector of the community for ordinary conversation.

(Ferguson, 1959a, p. 336)

In order to reach this definition, he looks at how the language works, specifically the following points: function, prestige, literary heritage, acquisition, standardization, stability, grammar, lexicon, and phonology. He saw how each of the two varieties works and drew his above-mentioned definition based on these points. Ferguson opened the door for research to look at aspects he did not discuss, such as the alternation between the two varieties and the social use of the varieties.

His research into Arabic resulted in several key articles analyzing the Arabic language. Ferguson (1959b) says that Arabic dialects today are a direct descendant from CA, which has been in use for a long time. He adds his contribution to this agreed-upon assumption and explains:

one important refinement to this hypothesis, namely that most modern Arabic dialects descend from the earlier language through a form of Arabic, called here the koine,[3] which was not identical with any of the earlier dialects and which differed in many significant respects from Classical Arabic but was used side by side with the Classical language during early centuries of the Muslim era.

(Ferguson, 1959b, p. 616)

He goes on to explain that what is called CA today existed side by side with other dialects in pre-Islamic times. It was the Arabic used in poetry and was the accepted form of standard Arabic among the Arabs of the peninsula at the time. Later on, with the advent of Islam, the use of this Arabic became accepted as the norm for written and formal Arabic. In other words, there was more than one variety of Arabic in the pre-Islamic times; the dialects of today come not only from the Classical Arabic used in the Quran but also one can trace elements from other pre-Islamic dialects that formed the early koine for Arabic. Ferguson explains that the formal variety and the spoken variety can be seen as high and low varieties based on the points he discusses. It is important to remember that this does not mean that the low is less or beneath the high, it is meant as a way to separate the varieties (Ferguson, 1959b).

The CA of the religion is written; it is one form that is used by all users of CA. Spoken varieties are spoken, and there are several dialects that differ according to factors such as location, age, education, and gender. The difference between spoken varieties can be so significant that it might even become difficult for speakers from one country to understand the local dialect of another speaker who is not from the same country. It can become incomprehensible, especially with the geographical distance, to understand the dialects not heard frequently. It is not possible to consider one spoken variety as the main variety and the other subsidiary since there are as many Arabic dialects as there are Arabic communities. Researchers have grouped dialects into five major groups: Maghrebi, Egyptian,

Levantine, Iraqi, and the Peninsula dialects. This division is based on the geographical location of the dialects and only covers the broader groups, but these groups can be divided into several subgroups or dialects where each dialect has its own intonation and stress patterns, pronunciation, vocabulary, and grammar.

Linguists continued to analyze language usage and tried to explain diglossia in more detail after Ferguson started this distinction. Studies followed that elaborated, agreed with, and often revised the work done by Ferguson. Research into the varieties of Arabic took another step in understanding how Arabic speakers use their language when Badawi (1973) looked at the language spoken in Cairo and analyzed it. Badawi looked at the language use from a sociolinguistic perspective and built on what Ferguson and other linguists stated earlier about how the Arabic language functions. Badawi looked at how Arabic is used in Cairo, the capital of Egypt and one of the largest cities in the Arab World. He examined the language usage of this large community. Cairene Egyptian Arabic gives a clear picture of how the Arabic language works in the real world from which Badawi established five levels of contemporary Arabic that are used today in any Arabic speaking community (see Section 2.3).

2.3 Levels of Arabic and Arabic usage

When diglossia is explained, it is crucial to keep in mind that even though there are two varieties of Arabic, a formal and an informal variety, this does not mean that only the classical and dialect varieties exist. The move from CA to dialect is on a continuum; Arabic is one language whether written or spoken. It is one social continuum where native speakers use a specific variety to reflect the social interaction they are doing or the educated level they belong to. There is a social breakdown of the language from CA to the local variety used by an average native speaker. Not all speakers of Egyptian Arabic in Cairo use the same intonation, vocabulary, or grammar. Not only are there the geographical varieties we mentioned earlier, but there are also social varieties in the one geographical variety. As mentioned above, Badawi (1973) described the linguistic situation of Arabic in Egypt, analyzing the language in Cairo and dividing it into five "levels":

1. Classical Arabic (CA) – "high"
2. Modern Standard Arabic (MSA) – "high"
3. Colloquial of the Educated and Cultured – "high"
4. Colloquial of the literate – "low"
5. Colloquial of the illiterate – "low"

(Badawi, 1973, p. 89)

CA, the language of religion and religious texts, has kept its "high" and "respected" place and has not changed since the beginning of Islam, more than 1,400 years ago. Yet, the average person does not speak it to conduct everyday business; it is a variety that has specific contexts to be used in. MSA is the language used in the media, newspapers, and books. It is formal Arabic but is not necessarily fully vocalized, and diacritics are not added to the printed words. MSA is the standard variety that is taught in schools, which is understood and used all across the Arab World. The standard varieties, CA and MSA, are both taught at schools, not acquired at home as is the case of spoken dialects. The difference between the classical language of religion and the colloquial language of the uneducated native speaker is huge. In between this spectrum are more levels of Arabic: language of the newspapers and journalism, of the university academic, of the professional engineer, of the laborer, of the handy man, and of others. They all share one dialect, but there are different levels according to the user of the language. The location, education, gender, and age of the speaker are all factors in the use of the dialect. The dialects also change with time: the language used by the older generation is different than the younger generation.

From a careful look at the levels of Arabic, we can see the similarity between 1 and 2 and the "high" variety described by Ferguson, while 4 and 5 are the "low" variety and three is a level in the middle. This middle level can be seen as closer to the higher levels, but as it has dropped features from MSA, it is less formal. In fact, it is the informal language of the educated so that it has features of formal language in it but is not strong enough to be considered a formal variety. Usually, a native speaker would use level 1 for prayers and in religious sermons, and use level 3, 4, or 5 for their conversation. The printed material, newspapers, magazines, and books are written in MSA, which is level 2. When native speakers write, they use MSA. Yet, over the last decade more and more people have been using colloquial words in printed form. This is a relatively new phenomenon. The reasons have been attributed to the wide use of social media; however, there are no studies at the moment to explain why there is a change in the written form. The point here is that CA does not change. MSA allows change, in which new words (from dialect) are incorporated into the language. The change might take time and the process takes time, but at the end of the day MSA does change while CA does not.

The Arabic terms Badawi uses to describe CA and MSA are *fuShat*[4] of heritage and *fuShat* of modern age. For the average native speaker of Arabic, this distinction is usually not clear. The distinction between these two levels is not seen by most native speakers, including highly educated speakers (Parkinson, 1991). They can use the language correctly, without distinguishing between the two levels. It is important to know these levels in a language learning situation so that the correct level of language is used in the correct situation. It would be totally inappropriate, for example, to use CA when buying groceries, or using illiterate colloquial words or sentence structure when writing in formal Arabic. The Arabic language can be considered to have a high variety that has native "users," not native "speakers" as no native speakers speak CA all the time. They use CA in the designated CA situations (mainly the religious context), and they use their local dialect for all non-religious purposes. Native speakers use a dialect to communicate and when the situation arises, they use the high variety to fulfill a specific function. This explains how all Arabs speak at least two varieties based on the language function.

Based on what has been discussed above, Muslims outside the Arab World can be said to be users of CA, the highest variety of Arabic. They learn in a formal setting, but the other levels in the continuum of Arabic is absent in their case. They understand CA to various degrees, depending on the formal learning of Arabic they had. They may not fully understand the language, but they use it to recite the verses of the Quran and they use this variety in their prayers. This common use of language of prayer, as well as the common belief, makes Muslims all over the world share a common culture. Muslims have more in common with the HLL than the non-HLL of Arabic. The fact that Muslim and Arabic culture overlap makes the Muslim language learner of Arabic a Muslim Heritage Language Learner (M-HLL) (see Section 5.2.1).

2.4 Arabic dialects

The five levels of Arabic represent the social levels used by native speakers in one specific place. Yet, the Arab World covers a large geographic area from the Atlantic Ocean in the west to the Persian Gulf in the east. The same social and functional divisions are present across the Arab World, but the people do not speak the same dialect; there are regional dialects. Researchers have grouped the dialects into five major groups: Maghrebi, Egyptian, Levantine, Iraqi, and the Peninsula dialects.

Both dialect and diglossia are aspects of the language where the HLL and the non-HLL differ. The fact of the matter is that the HLL is aware of diglossia and dialect. This is part of his home environment: the family speaks the dialect used in their country of origin. Most of the HLLs who have no formal education of Arabic but speak a dialect regard their knowledge of Arabic as incomplete, and very often register in the Arabic for Beginners class. They recognize and can speak an Arabic dialect, which is very different than listening to the news in MSA; in addition, they cannot read, so as a result, they see themselves as total beginners (see Section 5.2). Language learners usually ask about the most recommended dialect to learn; they are told it depends on their interest in the Arab World and which countries they are more interested in or plan to visit. The most commonly taught dialects are Egyptian Arabic and Levantine, and in recent years there has been an increased interest in Iraqi Arabic.

Another point that seems to be important to learners is knowing which dialect is the closest dialect to CA and whether or not the Arabic of the Arabian Peninsula is the closest dialect to CA and MSA. Learners usually think of the dialects of the Arabian Peninsula as one dialect but this is far from true. There have always been dialects within the Peninsula and these dialects can be divided into two linguistic groups that correspond with the inhabitants: the Bedouin dialects and the "sedentary" dialects. Holes (Holes, 2006) explains that the Arabic dialects in the Arabian Peninsula have maintained a number of CA linguistic features on different levels: on noun morphology, verb morphology, and syntax. He illustrates how the spoken dialects in Arabia, for example, use *tanween* (a grammatical ending for indefiniteness used in CA, but not in the spoken dialects outside Arabia). These retained features from CA are what often give the impression that the Arabic dialects in the Arabian Peninsula is CA not a dialect. This general impression is also found among the average native speakers of Arabic outside the Peninsula. So, for example, many Egyptians assume that the spoken Arabic of Saudi Arabia is the "correct" CA that they should use. Dialects differ from MSA or CA on more than one level; there are phonological, morphological, syntactical, and lexical differences between the dialects and MSA or CA.

Another point to share with the ALL is that Arabic was spoken first in the Arabian Peninsula and then spread further with Islam mainly and, to a certain extent, with trade (see Sections 3.2 and 3.3). The question of how many dialects Arabic has is not an easy question to answer, as there is no straightforward answer to give. Dialects can be looked at on a regional level, where there are five large dialect groups: the Maghrebi, Egyptian, Levantine, Iraqi, as well as the Peninsula dialects. Add to this other dialects with large numbers of users such as the Sudanese, Hassaniya (in Mauritania), and so on. In each of these groups, there are smaller regional dialects. Regional dialects are not unique to Arabic. Many languages have regional dialects, including English and French. Two things to remember when looking at Arabic dialects: first, how these dialects came to be; second, the vast geographical location where the language is used. With the spread of Islam outside the Arabian Peninsula, the locals in the new Muslim lands did not immediately adopt Arabic as their daily spoken language. Local languages were used for a while, and eventually Arabic took over in most (not all) these lands. The local languages had a significant influence on the Arabic spoken in the countries where it was adopted. Until the present day there are still traces of the pre-Arabic time in these dialects. This is clear in all dialects: Egyptian Arabic has traces of Coptic, Levantine Arabic has traces from the Aramaic language, and Maghreb dialects show the strong influence of Amazigh languages.

Due to the vast geographical area of the present-day Arabic-speaking population, the dialects are quite different from each other. The presence of a large number of dialects means there is vast difference on many levels, in phonology, vocabulary, and grammar. The dialects are so different to the extent that a Moroccan speaker might not be understood by a Syrian, and both speakers often resort to MSA in order to achieve complete understanding of one another. If we look at Arabic in Africa, the major dialects are Amazigh, Egyptian, and Sudanese in the Arab States, while there are minority speaking populations in a number of African countries such as Nigeria, Chad, and Ghana (see Section 3.2.1). Yet, to say that there is one Arabic-Maghrebi dialect is far from being accurate; the Arabic-Maghrebi dialect runs across North Africa from Morocco in the west to Siwa Oasis – in the very west of Egypt. Similarly, Egyptian Arabic is not one dialect: Cairene Egyptian Arabic in the north (known as Lower Egypt) is quite different than Aswani Egyptian Arabic in the south (known as Upper Egypt), for example. They differ on many levels even though they are clearly understood by all Egyptians; it can be a difference in intonation or vowel use on verbs that distinguishes a person from Alexandria from a person from Suez or Cairo. This adds another dimension to the language variety that learners, both HLL and non-HLL,

Arabic language(s) in the Arab World 25

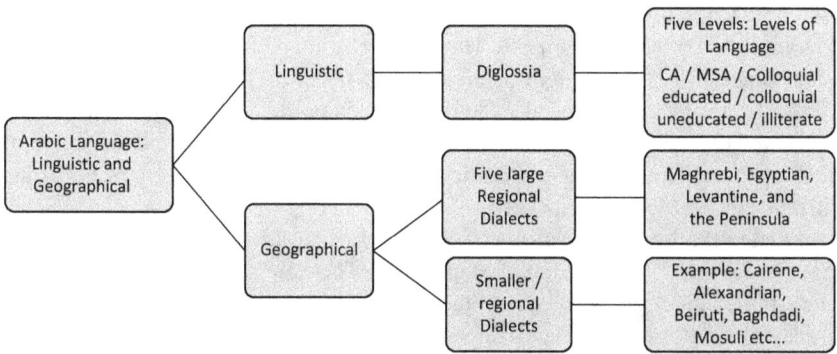

Figure 2.1 Chart showing social and geographical representation of the Arabic language

need to consider when learning Arabic. Usually for the HLL the issue of which dialect to learn is based on their family background.

Figure 2.1 outlines how Arabic can be looked at depending on the usage and language level, or the geographical areas where the language is used. It shows that for the language user, there are two factors that go hand in hand to determine the Arabic of the user: the social level and the geographical location.

2.5 Arabic in the Arab World

The Arabic language is spoken by all member states of the Arab League, of which there are 22.[5] Arabic is the official (or co-official) language of the member states of the Arab League, as well as being a co-official language in Eritrea, an observer state in the Arab League (The Arab League Official Webpage). There are six countries that recognize Arabic as a national language (Mali, Niger, Senegal) or minority language (Cyprus, Iran, Turkey). Maltese is often treated as a variety of Arabic for historical reasons (see Section 3.3.1). This makes the number of countries speaking Arabic higher than 28. One fact that learners need to be reminded of is that neither Iran nor Turkey are Arabic countries – they are not a member of the Arab League. Persian uses the Arabic script to write the language (as does Urdu and other languages). Ottoman Turkish was written in Arabic, but this changed in 1928 when Latin script was adopted to write Turkish as part of greater changes in modern Turkey. The language in Iran is Persian, but Arabic is a minority language in the country, and it is used as the language of religion. The same applies to Turkey and other Muslim states where Arabic is a language of religion.

2.6 Arabic language in Israel: A special status

In the case of Arabs in Israel this is a case where political reasons make Arabic a minority language and make native speakers become bilinguals. Arabs living in

Israel form 21 percent of the population according to the 2017 census of Israel; they are Arabs by ethnicity, and they are Israeli by citizenship. The status of Arabic in Israel is a unique case. The Arabic language had been an official language since the establishment of the State of Israel in 1948 until 2018 (Jewish Virtual Library, n.d.). Arabic used to be the second official language in Israel after Hebrew. This recently changed and Hebrew became the only official language of the State. Arabic is no longer an official language in Israel, yet 21 percent of the citizens are Arabic native speakers.

Article 4 in the Israeli Nation-State law published in *The Times of Israel* now reads as follows: "Article four – Language: A. The state's language is Hebrew. B. The Arabic language has a special status in the state; regulating the use of Arabic in state institutions or by them will be set in law. C. This clause does not harm the status given to the Arabic language before this law came into effect" (Wootliff, 2018). It is not clear what changes will come to the Arabic language, if any, after this law. The written form of Arabic was used in many official establishments before the change of the law, even though the translation was not always accurate (Harel-Shalev, 2006). At times, Arabic was missing, for instance a passport is issued in Hebrew and English but has never been issued in Arabic even when Arabic had an official language status. Arabs in Israel speak a Palestinian Arabic dialect and schools teach MSA to the students, as well as Hebrew. Many of HLLs coming to language classes in the West are of Palestinian descent whose families have immigrated to the West.

On the other hand, Arabic is the official language of the Palestinian authority. It is a member of the Arab League and Arabic is the only official language of the Gaza Strip and the Palestinian territories (The Arab League Official Webpage). Nevertheless, many Palestinians from the West Bank and Gaza need to learn Hebrew, especially if they cross the border to work in Israel. They are not a minority group in the Gaza Strip, but they still need to be bilinguals.

2.7 Minority languages in the Arab World

When people talk about language in the Arab World, they are talking about Arabic; but there are minorities in the Arab World who speak a language at home and another in the street. It would be incomplete to leave this chapter about Arabic without pointing out that there are non-Arabic languages, minority languages, in the Arab World. A number of these languages have been present since before Arabic was spoken in a specific region, such as Amazigh or Nubian in North Africa and the south of Egypt; on the other hand, some languages came to the region when their speakers moved to the Arab World, such as Armenian in Lebanon, Syria, and Egypt. The larger minority languages across the Arab World are Kurdish, Amazigh, and Somali. The smaller groups of languages include Armenian, Nubian, Siwi, Swahili, and Assyrian (also called Neo-Aramaic). Minority languages are found in countries across the whole of the Arab World. In North Africa, Amazigh is used; in Iraq and Syria, Kurdish is used; and in the Horn of Africa, Somali is used. Smaller minority groups can be found, such as Nubian in Egypt or Armenian in Lebanon, Syria, and Egypt.

The minority languages in the Arab World differ, not only in the number of users but also how much they are influenced by Arabic. Among the smaller groups of minority languages is Siwi, the Amazigh dialect used in the Oasis of Siwa to the west of Egypt; it is a minority language with the nearest oasis being 350 kilometers away, and it is spoken by a small population of about 15,000 native Siwans (Souag, 2009). The remote location of the oasis has meant that it kept its own identity; a Tuareg desert identity. The Siwi language is a variety of Amazigh and is as far east as the Amazigh language goes. The Siwans have their own Amazigh language, but this has been affected by Arabic in vocabulary and phonology. The men can be bilingual, but most of the women (especially the older generation) speak only Siwi as they do not need to communicate with people from outside the oasis. They have always lived in Siwa, from olden times, and have maintained their identity, including their language. Siwi shows the influence of Arabic, but not all minority languages have been influenced by Arabic. For example, Armenian has not been influenced by Arabic.

The Armenian language as a minority language came to the Arab World when Armenians left their homeland for political reasons. The Armenian community is a Christian community that migrated to different Arab countries in waves over a period of time for various reasons. They migrated to Syria and Lebanon as far back as during the Umayyad times, but the massive move came in the early twentieth century. The Ottoman Empire exiled them to the Arab lands under British or French mandate (Hovannisian, 1974). There is a difference between the earlier Armenians who migrated to the Arab World and the twentieth-century Armenians who moved to Lebanon. The latter group maintained their identity and had their schools, stores, and community clubs. Hovannisian (1974) points out that they regarded themselves of a higher caliber than the locals in Lebanon; they kept their own language and spoke a broken Arabic dialect. Another migrant destination for Armenians was Egypt. The Armenians came to Egypt as far back as the Roman and Byzantine times. In the nineteenth century, they became an important part in the close circle to the rulers. They had high political posts and some industries were in the monopoly of the Armenians (such as shoemaking and tobacco). Again, they maintained their identity and their language, they built Armenian schools and clubs, and they did not mix a lot with the Egyptians. Even today, the small remaining group of Armenians speak their language (but can read and write Arabic), keep their Armenian names, and go to the Armenian schools. They are not seen as a challenge or threat to society; they are accepted as a group that immigrated in a time of need and have become part of the society.

A very different minority language found in the Arab World is the Kurdish language. It is the language spoken by one of the larger ethnic groups in the Middle East and has two main dialects. As Rubin explains, it is difficult to have an exact number of the Kurdish speakers, as they are scattered over several countries, as well as in diaspora (Rubin, 2003). In the Arab World, they are found mainly in Iraq (4.5 million) and Syria (1 million). There have been successful calls for recognizing the Kurdish minority and their right to use their language. In Iraq, the 2013 Constitution stated in Article 4 that the Arabic language and the Kurdish language are the two official languages of Iraq. The Kurds differ from the Armenians in that they are mostly Muslims, and one of their man dialects uses Arabic script (even though the language itself is Indo-European). The Kurds do not have a country to return to, their territories are divided across political borders, and this is what makes this minority different from other minority groups and languages in the Arab World.

Arabic is a non-native, second language, for speakers of minority languages in the Arab World; they learn Arabic to communicate outside their community and in the streets. Yet, if they move to Europe or North America, their children become HLLs. This can be seen in the case of students from Amazigh background in Montreal. They are in the heritage class, even though they maintain an Amazigh identity (see Section 5.4.1). They see themselves as a separate ethnic group, and they are that; but at the same time, they have a bond or a link to Arabic through regional geography. Although this link might be religious or geographic, they choose to learn the language that their parents spoke as a second language outside the home. Unlike their parents who had to learn Arabic to communicate outside their community, these HLL choose to learn Arabic, while maintaining their Amazigh identity.

Notes

1 The term variety is used in a loose sense here; register is a similar term that can also be used.
2 A non-profit organization in Washington DC, http://www.cal.org/who-we-are/our-founder.
3 Definition of the term "koine" according to Merriam-Webster online dictionary: "a dialect or language of a region that has become the common or standard language of a larger area." https://www.merriam-webster.com/dictionary/koine
4 The term *fuSha* can be loosely translated to the well-versed tongue/language. He refers to them as *fuShat al-turaath* and *fuSha* of *al-'aSr*.
5 The following are the official members of the Arab League: Algeria, Bahrain, Comoros, Djibouti, Egypt, Iraq, Jordan, Kuwait, Lebanon, Libya, Mauritania, Morocco, Oman, Palestine, Qatar, Saudi Arabia, Somalia, Sudan, Syria, Tunisia, the United Arab Emirates, and Yemen. Arabic is also widely spoken in different countries in Africa, such as Eritrea. Arabic is a co-official language in a number of countries such as Israel and Chad.

Bibliography

Badawi, S. M. (1973). *Mustawayiat al-'arabiyya al-mu'asira fi misr* [The levels of contemporary Arabic in Egypt]. Cairo, Egypt: Dar al-Ma'arif.

Demeke, G. (2001). The Ethio-Semitic languages (Re-examining the classification). *Journal of Ethiopian Studies*, *34*(2), 57–93.

Ferguson, C. (1959a). Diglossia. *Word*, *15*(2), 325–340.

Ferguson, C. (1959b). The Arabic koine. *Language*, *35*(4), 616–630.

Harel-Shalev, A. (2006). The status of minority languages in deeply divided societies: Urdu in India and Arabic in Israel—A comparative perspective. *Israel Studies Forum*, *21*(2), 28–57. Retrieved from http://www.jstor.org/stable/41804950.

Holes, C. (2006). The Arabic dialects of Arabia. *Proceedings of the seminar for Arabian studies*, *36*, 25–34.

Hovannisian, R. (1974). The ebb and flow of the Armenian minority in the Arab Middle East. *Middle East Journal*, *28*(1), 19–32. Retrieved from http://www.jstor.org/stable/4325183.

Jewish Virtual Library. (n.d.). *American-Israeli cooperative enterprise (AICE)*. Retrieved March 2019, from https://www.jewishvirtuallibrary.org/latest-population-statistics-for-israel.

League of Arab States. (2017, Januiary). League of Arab States – economic sector. Retrieved May 2018, from Department of Statistics and Database http://www.ainportal.org/ar/SiteAssets/Lists/Statistics/AllItems/LAS_Stat_2017.pdf.

Parkinson, D. (1991). Searching for modern Fug for p://exampformal Arabic. *Al-'Arabiyya*, *24*, 31–61.

Rubin, M. (2003). Are Kurds a pariah minority? *Social Research*, *70*(1), 295–330. Retrieved from http://www.jstor.org/stable/40971614.

Souag, L. (2009). Siwa and its significance for Arabic dialectology. *Zeitschrift für Arabische Linguistik*, JSTOR, *51*, 51–75.

Wexler, P. (1980). Problems in monitoring the diffusion of Arabic into West and Central African languages. *Zeitschrift Der Deutschen Morgenländischen Gesellschaft*, *130*(3), 522–556.

Wootliff, R. (2018, July 18). *Final text of Jewish nation-state law, approved by the Knesset early on July 19*. Retrieved May 2019, from https://www.timesofisrael.com/final-text-of-jewish-nation-state-bill-set-to-become-law/.

Additional References

Al-Kahtany, Abdallah H. (1997). The "problem" of diglossia in the Arab world. *Al-'Arabiyya*, *30*, 1–30.

Bassiouney, R. (2009). *Arabic sociolinguistics: Topics in diglossia, gender, identity, and politics*. Washington, DC: Georgetown University Press.

Bulakh, Maria, & Kogan, Leonid (2011). Arabic influences on Tigre: A preliminary evaluation. *Bulletin of the School of Oriental and African Studies, University of London*, *74*(1), 1–39. JSTOR. Retrieved from www.jstor.org/stable/41287922.

Franjié, L. (2012). The "clash of perceptions" in Canada since 9/11: A study of the Canadian Arab community's communications. *International Journal*, *67*(4), 915–929. Retrieved from http://www.jstor.org.lib-ezproxy.concordia.ca/stable/42704939.

Freeman, A. (1996). Perspectives on Arabic diglossia. Retrieved from http://www.innerbrat.org/Andyf/Articles/Diglossia/digl_96.htm (Placeholder1).

Jazayery, M. (1970). The Arabic element in Persian grammar: A preliminary report. *Iran*, *8*, 115–124. doi: 10.2307/4299637.

Kamusella, T. (2017). The Arabic language: A Latin of modernity? *Journal of Nationalism, Memory & Language Politics*, *11*(2), 117–145.

Knappert, J. (1993). The Kurds: A brief history. *International Journal on World Peace*, *10*(2), 67–70. Retrieved from http://www.jstor.org/stable/20751890.

Miller, C. (2003) Linguistic policies and language issues in the Middle East. Usuki A. & H. Kato. In *Islam in the Middle Eastern studies: Muslims and minorities*, JCAS Symposium Series 7 (pp. 149–174), Osaka, Japan, halshs-00150396.

Owens, J. (2001). Arabic sociolinguistics. *Arabica*, *48*(4), 419–469. Retrieved from http://www.jstor.org.lib-ezproxy.concordia.ca/stable/4057667.

Owens, J. (2001). Creole Arabic: The orphan of all orphans. *Anthropological Linguistics*, *43*(3), 348–378.

Palmer, J. L. (2007). Arabic diglossia: Teaching only the standard variety is a disservice to students. *Arizona Working Papers in second Language Acquisition and Teaching*, *14*, 111–122.

Parkinson, D. (1991). Searching for modern Fuṣḥa: Real-life formal Arabic. *Al-'Arabiyya*, *24*, 31–64.

Qutbuddin, T. (2007). Arabic in India: A survey and classification of its uses, compared with Persian. *Journal of the American Oriental Society*, *127*(3), 315–338.

Rendsburg, G., Rubin, A., & Huehnergard, J. (2008). A proper view of Arabic, Semitic, and more. *Journal of the American Oriental Society*, *128*(3), 533–541. Retrieved from http://www.jstor.org.lib-ezproxy.concordia.ca/stable/25608410.

Rosenhouse, J. (2008). A new approach to the description of contemporary Arabic dialects (mainly in Israel). *Zeitschrift für Arabische Linguistik*, *48*, 35–57. Retrieved from http://www.jstor.org/stable/43525827.

Shohat, E. (2015). The question of Judeo-Arabic. *The Arab Studies Journal*, *23*(1), 14–76. Retrieved from http://www.jstor.org.lib-ezproxy.concordia.ca/stable/44744899.

Snir, R. (2006). "Arabs of the Mosaic Faith": Chronicle of a cultural extinction foretold. *Die Welt des Islams*, *46*(1), 43–60. New Series. Retrieved from http://www.jstor.org/stable/20140706.

3 Arabic beyond the Arab World

3.0 Introduction

Chapter 3 continues discussing the Arabic language. It looks at Arabic outside the Arab World in diverse societies, both in the East and West. This chapter focuses on where Arabic culture has (or had) a noticeable presence. It starts by looking at the relation between language and religion, it looks at both the Muslim and the Arab Worlds to see where they both overlap and where they differ. The Arabic language is the written language of the Quran; this creates a special relation between the Arabic language and the Muslim believer. Arabic is unique in that it is part of the cultural heritage of Muslims all over the world, even when it is not necessarily their mother tongue. Belief, Islam in this case, is part of the culture, and Arabic is the sole medium of expression of this belief and as such it becomes essential to the Muslim World. Even when Arabic is not the mother tongue of a community, it is still part of the people's everyday life and their unique cultural heritage. The language can be present, in the oral and written forms, together with the local, native culture in the non-Arab Muslim World. This is followed by an overview of the Arab immigrant community in North America and Europe; a short summary of how this community grew is given in order to see where the Arabic language is present. The last part looks at how the presence of Arabic is seen in the West, how the society and the media view and often use Arabic. A brief discussion of how Arabic words have come into English in the present day, in the form of religious and political terms as well as in the use of Arabic proper names, is given in the final section. By the end of this chapter the reader will have seen where outside the Arab World the Arabic language is used – whether as a mother tongue, as a heritage language, or as a language of religion.

The chapter does not look at language learners (see Chapter 5 for the HLLs of Arabic), it focuses on the Arabic language and how it is present in different and diverse communities; it explains what role(s) it plays and shows how it differs from one place to another.

3.1 Arabic and religion

Islam is one of the major world religions, second after Christianity, with approximately 1.5 billion followers (Berkley Center for Religion, Peace and World,

2019). This chapter presents the role of Arabic in a select number of places where there are Muslim communities as an example of how and where Arabic is used. The aim is to give an overall representation from different parts of the world to see how the language is used and how different people use the language in different ways.

The majority of the Muslim population is not Arab nor from the Arab World, yet all Muslims use Arabic in their prayers. According to the Berkley Center for Religions, Peace and World Affairs (2019), only 20 percent of Muslims are of Arabic background. Non-Arab Muslims use Arabic as a language of religion, and at times a language for basic communication such as greetings or in other situations where the formulaic use of the language is used. The pronunciation of the speakers is not necessarily native-like, and the language used is CA or MSA. The Arabic language has a special status in the Muslim World, as it is the language of the religion, which is part of the identity of the individual. Muslims come from all corners of the globe; they differ in race, mother tongue, and traditions (some elements overlap) but they share a common faith that is manifested through different means and one of these means is the Arabic language. The faith becomes part of a common culture they all share. For Muslims, religion is not only the verses they recite, it is a way of life they follow. This way of life that is regarded as part and parcel of the religion means that all Muslims share not just the prayers in one language, but also, they all share common values and a unifying "culture" (more of a way of life here) that they all agree to live by.

A formal definition of culture can be found in references, and there have been publications under the title "What is Culture?" going back more than one hundred years (Buckham, 1892; MacDonald, 1991; Granbery, 1929). MacDonald talks about how intercultural understanding is underdeveloped and how people need to not only speak other languages, but also understand the ways of life and values and worldviews of other cultures; he says: "Culture may be understood as a consortium of communication (or a bundle of messages) that a given people have in common: their shared experiences, shared perceptions and values, shared consciousness" (MacDonald, 1991, p. 10). This can apply to the Muslim World as much as it applies to any culture. There are Muslim values that all the Muslims share in addition to the unique ethnic values that each separate group of Muslims has.

The Arab World covers a large geographic area with groups and sub-groups of Arabs that might not all share the same exact culture. Defining the culture of the Muslim World is not an easy task. The Muslim World is quite diverse, and it reaches the far southeast of Asia, passing by different groups of Muslims along the way. It is not easy to define what is meant by a Muslim culture, if there is one culture that the Muslim World shares. There are factors such as geographical distances, language barriers, history, and others that can result in the presence of more than one culture. Islam has an influence on political life, social customs, architecture, and the development of the arts. This is why Muslim culture, which includes Arabic culture, is seen in non-Arabic places, in Europe, Asia, and Africa. Popovic and Rashid point out that both the physical and the written culture in the Balkans reveal Muslim culture between the sixteenth and eighteenth centuries during the Ottoman era (Popovic and Rashid, 1997). This is manifested in Ottoman architecture of mosques, bridges, and fountains in all of their artistic features. There were famous poets, prose writers, and historians writing in Arabic and Turkish. At the time, the educated could write in Arabic, Turkish, and often Persian. Also present is the oral and written culture, where Arabic words are present such as *miiezzin/mu'adhdhin*[1] and *mahkeme/mahkamah*.[2] The point is that culture is more than one thing; it is physical in the form of buildings and writings as well as traditions that are transmitted from one generation to another.

In a short article Ram (1997) says that "culture is not a static category to be brought or imported and lived on for all the times to come. The interaction of social groups and changing socio-political scenario keep it constantly on the move" (Ram, 1997, p. 310). One cannot bring a culture and impose it on a place. The same religion can have different faces in different places according to the social, political, or economic situation. The core values are the same, but the manifestation can be different depending on the place. Ram discusses how Islam entered India and how it started in the south due to the interaction with Muslim traders. Later, during invasions, people converted out of fear or in anticipation of rewards, and many of the poor converted to escape religious authorities or priests. Ram does not discuss the Muslim culture in detail; his aim is to explain that Muslims in India are Indians and their Muslim culture is a Muslim-Indian culture. Although he does not discuss language in his article, he refers to places that have Arabic names in Mumbai, such as Hajj Ali; he talks about Allah using the Arabic/Muslim term. So, again, language is seen as part of the culture of the Muslims, even if they are not Arabs themselves.

One way to look at it is to consider religion as one big umbrella under which all Muslims are grouped, and following the religion makes it a core part of the culture. It includes all that is acceptable by Muslims across the Muslim World, even though it can be reflected differently in different places. There are common religious and cultural grounds followed by Muslims – Arab and non-Arab alike. It is not just common prayers in one common language but also a common view toward material and non-material things. The culture can be influenced by the place, the people, and the time. In other words, Muslims share beliefs, traditions, and common elements in their culture; they also differ in certain traditions and cultural aspects depending on which part of the Muslim World they are located in. For example, family relations and extended family all being close is common across the Muslim World; so is sharing food during the fasting month of Ramadan, which is part of Muslim traditions. This is how religion becomes intertwined with tradition and culture. Dressing modestly or covering up for women is a religious requirement, but this is not done the same way across the Muslim World; it manifests itself differently in different Muslim countries as some are stricter in the required dress codes than others. The implementation of modesty is different, but the idea is agreed upon as part of the religion. Also, the rejection of tattoos or body piercings are examples of common grounds that stem from religious belief.

34 *Arabic as a heritage language*

Arabic is not only spoken by native Arabic speakers (in the Arab World or outside by immigrants), but also by Muslims in Muslim countries and communities outside the Arab World. Arabs use a local dialect, while non-Arabs use CA for religious purposes since they are readers of Arabic. Many also write, listen, and speak MSA. For many non-Arab Muslims, language is a part of their identity, as this is the language that expresses their faith and belief. The non-Arab Muslim might be regarded as an Arabic reader, even if they do not speak the language.

3.2 Arabic language and Muslim/non-Arab communities

Language does not spread in one single way; it is a process that occurs over time. The spread of Arabic outside the Peninsula is usually associated with the spread of Islam. Despite the fact that Arabic is the voice of the Quran, not all Muslims speak Arabic as a mother tongue, nor are all Arabs Muslim. This is a fact that many in the West do not recognize immediately and they tend to think that all Muslims are Arabs and vice-versa.

Arabic is spoken primarily in the Arab World, but there are Arabic speaking, non-immigrant minorities outside of the Arab World. The expansion of the Arabic territories in Asia and Africa from the early times of Islam, as well as the trade routes with Africa and Asia, has led to the presence of Arabic-speaking minorities in those regions. Muslims live on every continent in the globe. They do not all belong to one ethnic group; they come from all backgrounds. There are African Muslims, Asian Muslims, Indian Muslims, and others, they are not migrants. There are communities that converted to Islam centuries ago and maintained their heritage, as well as the Muslim heritage, thus creating a unique heritage that is African-Muslim, Chinese-Muslim, Indian-Muslim, etc. There are Muslim majority countries in Europe such as Bosnia, Albania, and Kosovo, as well as large Muslim communities in the Balkans that have been established and present since the tenth century. They maintain a Muslim identity and it is seen even in their architecture, traditions, and their names.

3.2.1 Arabic in Africa: Nigeria

Arabic has influenced African languages, and this can be seen in languages of countries with a noticeable Muslim population and in other languages in Africa as well. There is more than one reason for this language effect: first, there is the proximity of the southern part of the Arabian Peninsula to Africa; then, there are the trade relations that were present from the pre-Islamic times. The interactions between Arabic traders and East Africans, spanning centuries, resulted in Arabic having a significant influence on the language of Swahili, for example. A third influence is the nomadic movements of tribes crossing over from the Peninsula to Africa, where they would bring their language to the continent, and even when they did not share it with the native African tribes, eventually they intermarried and coexisted.

Africa is the second-most-populated continent, second only to Asia. The most populated country in Africa is Nigeria. Arabic has had a presence in Nigeria for a long time. It is not possible to point to the exact date that Arabic entered Nigeria, but the language came through traders, and then Islam came and required the knowledge of Arabic to fulfill the religious duties. Onireti and Abubakar (2012) point out another important factor that established Arabic in Nigeria: migration of some Arab tribes, such the Shuwas, to the country in the thirteenth century. The Shuwas are Arabic speakers and they speak an Arabic variety, known as Shuwa Arabic; they live a nomadic life raising cattle. They are also referred to as Baggara, from the Arabic word *bagar* meaning cow, since they are cattle herders. The Arabic presence in Nigeria continued to develop naturally, with tribal movement and religion, as well as with trade. This was before colonialism in the nineteenth century, which tried to remove the Arabic influences but failed. Present-day Nigeria is predominantly Muslim in the north and Christian in the south. The Arabic literary history is also present in Nigeria. It goes back 800 years with the poet and writer Abu Ishaq Ibrahim al-Kanemi who died c. 1212 (Hunwick, 1997).

Hausa, the largest ethnic group in Africa and Nigeria, used the Arabic script in their writing, referring to it as *Ajami*; later, Latin script was also used and referred to as *Boko*. The influence of Arabic in Nigeria is immense (Hunwick, 1997). Writings were produced in Hausa and, in the twentieth century, there were more and more works written in Arabic. There have always been writers, poets, and Arabic-Islamic teaching going back to the fifteenth century (Hunwick, 1997). This continued and a reform came over the Arabic-Islamic writings (both in verse and prose) in the nineteenth century, with large numbers of works produced in most of the Islamic disciplines, as well as secular and academic prose. There are well-recorded lists of different types of religious texts produced in Arabic in Nigeria including biography, Arabic language linguistics (including morphology, syntax, and lexicography), as well as jurisprudential literature – covering problem areas such as prayer, inheritance, and ritual purity. With Arabic printing houses available in Nigeria from the late 1940s, it became more accessible to print in Nigeria, rather than import books to teach about religion. Hunwick concludes that the number of Nigerian Arabic writers will increase, as the number of Muslims is increasing, and that the use of Arabic is changing with time as people travel more frequently now and the teaching of languages is different than in the past (Hunwick, 1997). The use of MSA has increased and is on a wider scale in Nigeria than before; there are communities where people converse in MSA, such as in the towns of Kano, Ilorin, Iwo, and Lagos (Onireti and Abubakar, 2012, p. 90).

Nigeria is an example of an African country where Arabic has been present as a language of religion for a long time and continues to be used today. In places where Arabic is the language of the minority group, the Arabs have to become bilingual. This is seen in several areas in Africa; for example, in Mauritania, the local Arabic *Hassaniya* dialect speakers had to become bilingual and use Wolof, which is the majority language (Wexler, 1980). This indicates that even if Arabic does have the prestige of being the religious language, it still has not replaced the African language of the area. Not only that, but Arabic has also influenced African languages, and we find Arabic vocabulary infiltrating into many of these languages (Wexler,

1980). This, as mentioned earlier, is because of trade, geographical proximity, as well as religion. Arabic has influenced names in Africa, so that not only the Baggar tribe name comes from Arabic; but also, the word *Swahili* is a plural adjectival form of the Arabic word *sahil* meaning "of the coast" (Venkatraman, 2015). Swahili is the language spoken along the eastern coast of Africa, and it started as a lingua franca that came to exist as a result of close trades between the tribes on the coast and the tribes on the other side of the Arabian Peninsula.

3.2.2 Arabic in Asia: Indonesia

In countries where the majority of the population is Muslim, the mother tongue is not necessarily Arabic. The largest Muslim country in the world is Indonesia, with a population of 271 million people (United Nations, 2019) and 99 percent of the population is Muslim, yet the only official language is Indonesian.

When people speak about Arabic and Islam in Asia, they are often referring to the southwestern corner of Asia, to the Arabian Peninsula, where people speak Arabic and are Muslims. But Islam has reached far beyond that corner in Asia; it has reached the South, Southeast Asia, and China. In all these places, it has maintained its distinct qualities, as well as become part of another culture. This developed over the centuries in different ways according to the conditions in the different countries. Arab traders and early Muslims from Persia and India had reached Southeast Asia since the seventh century. Whether it was in a Muslim majority country, such as Indonesia, or a Muslim minority country, such as Singapore, one of the first ways Islam spread was mainly by traders. Usually, it spread from the coast to the inlands in a quiet and natural, unresisted way (as it did in Africa). Houben (2003) explains that there were reciters among those traders who memorized the Quran in Arabic and then taught it to the new believers. Later, in the nineteenth century, the steamships brought the Muslims to Haj,[3] and Singapore became a hub for the journey. At that time, students who were educated in Al Azhar University in Cairo[4] started to translate and print articles in religious journals that Muslims could read. This is how the Arabic language came to establish a significant presence in that part of the world.

A detailed explanation of Arabic loanwords in Indonesian is given by Van Dam (2010). The language borrowed colloquial and CA words. This depended on the course of how Arabic reached the local population: was it through the traders or the Islamic teachers. The way these words came into Indonesian is not always clear, as he points out, partly because of the language reform that took place and aimed at creating a standardized Bahasa-Indonesia written form. At times, this meant making the Arabic dialect words closer to CA. Van Dam looks at the days of the week, how six of the seven come from CA: *Hari Ahad* (classical Arabic: *yawm ai-'ahad*), *Senin* (*al-'ithnayn*), *Selasa* (*al-thalathd*), *Komis* (*al-khamees*), *Jumaat* (*al-jum'ah*), and *Sabtu* (*al-sabt*) are all closer to the CA, but Wednesday is *Hari rabu*, which is closer to the Arabic Hadhramaut dialect in Yemen, where it is assumed many of the traders came from, with some even settling in Indonesia. This is the only example of colloquial Arabic in official Bahasa Indonesia.

Indonesian Muslims do not speak Arabic in everyday life today, yet they learn the basic Arabic they need for their religious practices and prayers. They also share a common religious culture with the whole Muslim world. The Muslim Indonesian language learners have a strong religious reason to learn the language. They learn it at schools in Indonesia and many language learners travel to Muslim countries, such as Egypt or Saudi Arabia, to continue their language and religious studies. They learn mainly CA and MSA, but not the dialect.

3.3 Arabic language and non-Muslim/non-Arab communities

Islam has been known to be one of the main reasons why the Arabic language spread outside the Arab World, as well as being the reason why the Arab World has extended outside the Peninsula. Arabic has in the past influenced languages of present non-Muslim communities outside the Muslim World. Historically, in places like Sicily and the South of Spain (Al-Andalus), the Arabic language was spoken when they were part of the Arab empire. Then, the speakers stopped using the language when the political reasons for using it were no longer present. The history of Arabic in these parts is not presented here, since these places no longer use Arabic and, as such, are not directly related to the Arabic language of today. The parts of Africa that are not on the coast, where traders did not reach, were not directly introduced to Arabic, but loanwords from Arabic are present in many of these languages through intermediary languages – whether African, Indian, or Persian.

3.3.1 Arabic in Malta: Semitic meets Romance

The case of Maltese is unique; Malta is not a Muslim country and it does not have a large Muslim community. Yet, Malta has close ties with North Africa and its historical ties with the Arab World go back many centuries. Malta is an island 60 miles south of Sicily and 200 miles north of Libya. Its history has been intertwined with the Arab-Islamic history through trade. Malta has always had a mixed heritage and people very often consider it Arabic, or at least, assume it has a large Arabic community.

When we look at the languages spoken in the Mediterranean basin, there is Arabic in North Africa, the European Languages in the south of Europe, and then there is Malta. Malta speaks Maltese, which is originally Semitic, and today is a hybrid from Italian (Romance) and Arabic (Semitic). As Agius (1981) points out, the Semitic part in the Maltese language is the than the Romance parts and is said to have had its roots in the island long before the Arabs occupied the islands (870–1091). Trade between the Arabs and Malta (and neighboring Sicily) have had a significant role on the language of Malta.

Maltese is seen by some linguists as a dialect of Arabic, this is mainly because it is a Semitic language with shared vocabulary with Arabic, especially the North African dialects. The language is a fusion of Norman (Latin), Greek and Arabic form the basis of the Maltese language. Researchers have noted that the Semitic base of the Maltese language remained strongly intact despite all the different occupiers who came to the island and tried to impose their language on the people. The language is similar to Arabic in vocabulary and many of the grammar rules, but it is written in Latin script. It is as if the Latin alphabet were superimposed on the Arabic-Semitic base (Fellman, 1982). Yet, it differs from Arabic in that it does not have two varieties, and thus there is no diglossia in Maltese, only the local dialect and no formal variety that is used to communicate on the formal level. When an average native speaker of Arabic hears Maltese, they can easily mistake it for a dialect of Arabic that they are not familiar with.

In more modern times, there was an ongoing war of languages on the island between English and Italian to become the official language of Malta. This was settled in 1934, when English was chosen with Maltese as the two official languages of the island. The Maltese people are Catholics and see themselves as Europeans. Despite that, the Maltese culture shares many Arabic features, for example, architecture, culinary habits, as well as the language. All of this explains why Malta is often thought of as a country closer to the Arab World than any other country in Europe.

3.3.2 Arabic in Ethiopia

There are other places where Islam did not reach the country and become the religion of the majority, but the language did have an impact on the people and the language. Ethiopia is a case in point. The effect of the Arabic language on Ethiopian languages did not come through Islam but is seen in a different way. Ethiopia has been a Christian land from the pre-Islamic times. Versteegh (2001) points out that the interaction with Arabic was different in Ethiopia than other parts of Africa. He explains that written Arabic words come in through the translation of Christian Arabic text mainly to Ge'ez (which later developed into present day Amharic). The Ethiopian Orthodox church has historically had special ties with the Coptic Orthodox Church in Egypt. Parts of the southern population became Muslims around the year 1000, and there was also minimal contact with Arabic traders scattered in different parts of the country. Arabic verbs that were integrated into Tigre are treated like Arabic verbs, this is due to the similarity between Arabic and Tigre, which is spoken by the Tigre in Eritrea (belongs to the North Ethiopic subdivision of the South Semitic languages).

Countries have borrowed from Arabic from before the time of Islam, such as in the Horn of Africa for example, which is the result of trade and geographic proximity. It is safe to say that religion is a key reason for the spread of the language, but it is not the only reason. The reasons for the spread of Arabic are important, but the main focus here is the elements of the language that spread outside the Arabic-speaking world and how these elements became part of the different languages.

3.4 Arabic in immigrant communities

In the modern times, Arabs have migrated out of the Arab World for different reasons including, but not limited to, political, religious, and economic. The historical reasons that led to the establishment of these communities will not be looked at, but rather the places where Arabs settled will be briefly outlined. The chapter looks at examples of these places, both in North America and in Europe, which include countries where Arab immigrant communities were established and are still present. It does not look at Arabic in South America or the more recent move of refugees to Eastern Asia for example. The book gives examples as an attempt to see the current state of the Arabic language outside the Arab and Muslim World.

3.4.1 Arabic immigrant communities in North America

The migration to the Americas came in waves. From the mid-nineteenth century, Arabic migrants from conflict areas in Greater Syria moved to the Americas, which has continued to the present day for different reasons. Toward the end of the century, educated Moroccans left for the US, as well as French-speaking Canada (Fargues, 2013). The Arab-American community is a diverse community, as diverse as the Arab World itself; the Arab World shares common unifying elements that make all the emigrants from this Arab World belong to one large group, with their sub-group being the country of origin. The Arab community speaks Arabic, has the same culture and the same traditions, but has regional variations that give each Arabic country its unique identity based on different factors. According to the Arab American Institute (Arab American Institute, 2019), the majority of the Arab-American community lives in metropolitan areas in California, Michigan, New York, Texas, and Florida. There are 3.7 million Arab-Americans and 82 percent of them are American citizens, with the majority American-born. This means that there is a large second- or third-generation Arabic community and this is the generation that is today seen to be trying to connect to its roots and to find its complete identity. One way of doing this is by learning the language of their parents or grandparents (see Section 5.1).

In Canada, the Arabic community has increased in numbers over the last two decades. Arabic speakers from North Africa and Lebanon were the first to move to Quebec. They were followed by Egyptians, who started going to Quebec 30 years ago; more recently, Syrians and Iraqis fleeing political conflict and war zones moved to Quebec. Today, Arabic is the third language spoken in Montreal (Statistics Canada, 2012). It is normal to walk in the streets of Montreal and hear different Arabic dialects spoken by different age groups. According to the Canadian Arab Institute[5] report on the Canada Census, the majority of Canadian Arabs (around 90 percent in 2010) live in the big cities, with Montreal having the largest Arab community in Canada, followed by Toronto, then Ottawa (Dajani, 2014). This is similar to the US where the Arab immigrants mostly live in big cities.

In Quebec, the French-speaking province in Canada, there appears to be a need to protect the French language from English, which is why there are language laws implemented to try to maintain the Francophone nature of the province. In 1977, the Charter of the French Language spelled out the detailed use of the French

40 Arabic as a heritage language

language in Quebec (Gouvernement du Québec, 2019). Over the last decade, the need to protect the Francophone from the Anglophone presence in the province became part of a bigger need: to protect Francophone culture from other foreign cultures, and this included the Muslim and Arab culture. Politicians in Quebec, as well as in some places in Europe, are very often threatened by the presence of the foreign culture in their own backyard and try to build defense mechanisms against the increased presence of the foreign culture. This is the case in Quebec, with the recent Bill 21 law, the secularism law, which is a controversial law that has been seen to target Muslim women who wear the hijab. In Quebec, what started as protecting the Francophones from the Anglophones is now becoming protecting the Francophones from the Anglophones, the Arabophones, the Muslims, and the "other" in general. The language policy in Quebec has not stopped the increase in the use of Arabic in immigrant communities, and with the increase in the number of Syrians and other Arabs coming to Quebec, this does not look to change in the near future.

The statistics on demographics show that there is a continuous increase in the number of immigrants from the Arab and Muslim World to North America and Europe. This can explain why there appears to be more HLLs in the Arabic classroom today than there were in the past. When looking at the official statistics one can see that the statistical data is gathered differently in different countries. For instance, in the US, the Middle East and North Africa (known as MENA) population are not always put together as one group, actually the US census has no ethnic group for Arab or Middle East identification. In an article for the Migration Policy Institute, Cumoletti and Batalova look at Arabic immigrants who are grouped under MENA, but are actually in the same group with immigrants from Turkey and Iran which makes the results inaccurate (Cumoletti and Batalova, 2018). Nevertheless, MENA data is the closest official record of Arab immigrant figures available. The MENA immigrant population in the US from 1980 to 2016 shows an increase from 223,000 in 1980 to 1,167,000 in 2016 (Figure 3.1). As the figures

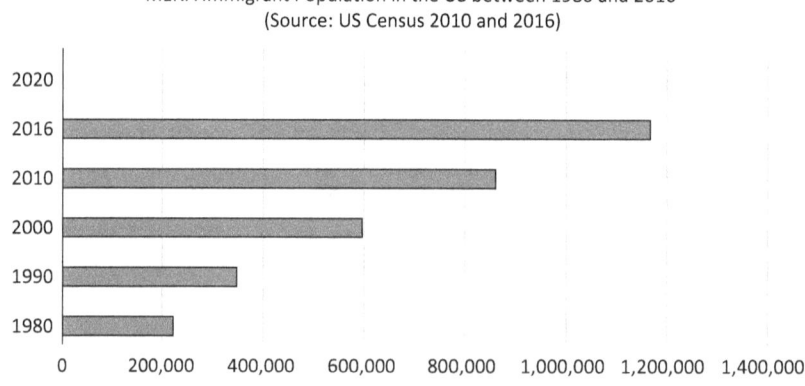

Figure 3.1 MENA immigrant population in the US between 1980 and 2016

show, there has been a large increase in the number of immigrants from this part of the world. While there has been a four-fold increase is size (1,167,000 in 2010 as opposed to 223,000 in 1980), an increase is also expected in the second and third generation of these immigrants wanting to learn Arabic.

As for Canada, the population of the country is almost one-tenth of the US's. Canada has a population of about 36 million while the US has a population of about 330 million[6]. This is why the numbers of speakers of Arabic in Canada are less than in the US, but the percentage of the speakers relative to the total population reveals that Arabic is one of the larger immigrant languages in Canada. A look at the Statistics Canada report shows that Arabic is among the top languages that saw an increase in the percentage of users of the language from 2000 to 2011. Actually, it is the third immigrant language with an increase of 46.8 percent following only Tagalog 64.1 percent and Mandarin 50.4 percent (Statistics Canada, 2012). It precedes other immigrant languages, such as Italian or German, in the increase in number of users. There are cities where Arabic is the most widely used immigrant language, such as in Montreal or Gatineau. In Montreal, Arabic and Spanish account for nearly one-third of the people speaking an immigrant language at home – 636,000 report speaking an immigrant language at home and of those 108,000 (17 percent) report speaking Arabic. This is an increase of 46.2 percent from the previous report.

3.4.2 Arabic immigrant communities in Europe: Denmark

The Arab World is the closest non-European neighbor to Western Europe, and this proximity has in the past, as well as in the present, been one of the reasons for the movement between Western Europe and the Arabic-speaking countries in both directions. In modern times, there has been movement across the Mediterranean for various reasons, such as Greeks moving to Lebanon in the early twentieth century. Then, after World War II and the shortage of labor in Europe, cheap labor migration from French-speaking North Africa to France was very common and was welcomed by the French. In North Africa, the migrants who left for Europe were labor much needed in Europe in the inter-war years in the twentieth century; then in the seventies these low-skilled laborers decided to stay and bring their family such as the Moroccan men (Fargues, 2013). In the seventies, Palestinians moved to Europe from Lebanon after the civil war (Nielsen, 2017). That was followed by different waves of immigration for different political, economic, and religious reasons. Arab immigration to Denmark has been increasing over the last decade, to the extent that the phenomenon has caused the public, non-government organizations, and the government to form opinions and develop their own agendas.

The use of the Arabic language by the Arabic immigrant community across Europe and how Europeans perceive the Arabic language are topics that need more research – but are beyond the scope of this book. Much of the information published about Arabic is concerned about the spread of the language and its users, and how this can change the face of Europe. This is reflected in the words of politicians who want to preserve the native language of the country from the "other" who is bringing a different language, religion, and culture to Europe – such as in France, Belgium, and Holland. This is similar to the language concerns in Quebec where the French Canadians are trying to maintain the Francophone nature of the province from the anglophones and more recently from the "other," or in other words "the Arab Muslim."

In the twentieth century, Arabic communities moved to countries across Europe at various times for different reasons. In this section, the Arabic language in Denmark is looked at as an example of how Arabic is perceived in Europe. The migrant Arabic community in Denmark is relatively new, and they are a representative of the present-day situation of the Arabic language in Europe. As Nielson (2017) explains, the first noticeable move of Arab immigrants to Denmark came from Morocco in the 1960s; later Palestinians came to Denmark to flee the civil war in Lebanon in the seventies. Then, at the turn of the century, more immigrants and refugees came to Denmark because of the war in Iraq and later the war in Syria. By 2015, there were about 100,000 Arab immigrants in Denmark – a country with a population of 5.7 million according to the 2015 census. This, as Nielson points out, makes Arabic the largest non-Western immigrant language in Denmark.

The increase in the number of speakers has meant that Arabic can be taught after school, as an additional heritage language. In high school there are currently ten secondary schools that offer Arabic as a foreign language for students in Denmark. Nielsen (2017) recognizes that teaching Arabic in secondary school does not continue from what has been taught in primary. In primary schools, Arabic is taught as a heritage language while in secondary schools it is taught as a foreign language – even though 90% of the students are from immigrant Arab families. She cannot explain the change of identification of the language, which she sees as a flaw in the system. Finally, at the university level there has been an obvious increase in the demand to study Arabic; from the 1990s until the present the figures have been at least four times higher (see Section 6.2).

3.5 Arabic as a language in the West

Earlier in the chapter, it was mentioned that there appears to be a general feeling of discomfort, or more, toward Arabic in the West at the present time. The reasons may vary, and can include the media, lack of education, and stereotyping. A number of politicians in Denmark have suggested banning the use of foreign languages in recess at primary schools, and banning the use of signs that are bilingual, so no more signs should be written in Arabic and Danish. These measures resemble what Quebec is doing with the French and English signs in the province. There have also been calls to stop providing free interpreters for immigrants after seven years of being in the country. One unexpected proposal from politicians in Denmark was to ban satellite dishes in order to stop the exposure to the channels that promote hatred to the continent – these include the Arabic channels Al Jazeera and Al Arabiya. Nielson (2017) says that this negative coverage of Arabic is only one way to look at Arabic and that Arabic can also be seen as a resource that Denmark has in our present global times. Denmark is a relatively small European country and in the case of Arabic there is a smaller scale in effect than in countries such as France, Italy, and Germany where the number of Arabs and Muslims is higher and the concern that Arabs and Arabic are spreading can be felt as greater. The perception of the Arabic language and how the media and politicians present it is often negative, and this can affect how it is used in these countries.

This tension between the Muslim World and the West is not new, historically there has been religious tension and even wars. Byrd (2017) talks about finding a common language with the Muslims and how this has been done in the past, for example in the time of the Fifth Crusades. He looks at the communication process, but not the verbal language between Europe from the times of the Crusades until now. He follows the Vatican and how it has sought, at different times, to find a "common language" with the Muslim Arab World. There have been attempts to use a "common language of a religious worldview, especially ones that share similar backgrounds and therefore theological presuppositions, i.e. the monotheistic faith of Abraham" (Byrd, 2017p. 10).

His conclusion is that people need to accept each other rather than change one another – the same way Pope Francis tries to accept and welcome Muslim refugees in Europe today. The Pope has made several attempts to try to stop and resolve the growing antagonism between Muslim immigrants in Europe and Europeans. He has called upon Catholics "to see them not as a threat to European culture, but as 'neighbors' in search of a helping hand and a better future for their children" (Byrd, 2017). This call by the highest Christian figure in the Catholic World shows that there is lack of communication between the Muslim and the Western World. This can be seen in the way that refugees from the Middle East and Africa are not welcomed, a large part of that is seen in the rejection of symbols of Islam, including the language – the Arabic language. This antagonism toward the language and its users is seen in different forms. The reasons for it may vary, but Nielsen (2017) has noted that the press often presents Arabic as a religious language or a simple language that is not fit for modern times. Also, many of the immigrants are from lower socioeconomic groups and as such are often seen as a burden on the taxpayer.

If, in the past, there was a need to find a common language to understand the Muslim World, today this need is even more felt. Outside the Muslim World, the Arabic language is foreign, strange, and often unwelcome. This can be seen today when speakers of the language feel profiled in Europe and in North America. The way the language is presented in Europe or North America makes the general public hesitant to accept the language and the speakers at times. This is why stories appear in newspapers about a speaker of Arabic being reported as suspicious on a plane, and subsequently asked off the plane. Reports about such incidents have been reported since 2006 and up to the present moment. For instance, in 2016, a UC Berkeley researcher was removed from a flight after a fellow passenger heard them speak Arabic on their phone. The passenger that reported the alleged threat said the speaker ended the call with the word "inshallah" (meaning

44 *Arabic as a heritage language*

"God willing") and the passenger thought that the speaker used the word "shahid," meaning "martyr," during the conversation. After being removed, the researcher was questioned by the FBI (Milman, 2016). This is the result of Islamophobia, or Arabophobia, and it shows how political reasons can make a language and its users be a cause of discomfort or even a threat.

3.5.1 *Arabic words in English in recent times*

Language borrowings happen all the time, often to fill a gap or to express a concept that is not available in one language. Historically, English borrowed words from Arabic such as *algebra, sugar, coffee, lemon*, among others. These words are no longer thought of as Arabic by the English speakers. More recently, there are words that are related to religion and politics that have come into English, and non-Muslims in the West recognize them as Muslim/Arabic words but are not necessarily sure what they mean. They are Arabic words that are seen as "Muslim Words" and have been used in English script to refer to Muslim concepts, values, or beliefs; these include terms such as *Allah* (God), *Ramadan* (Muslim fasting month), *halal* (religiously permitted to eat), *ummah* (nation), and *shari'ah* (Islamic law). Another term used in English is *jihad* (effort to fulfill the faith). This term has come into English with only one meaning, holy war; this is one of the meanings of the term *jihad* but not the most common, or only, meaning in Arabic. There are also phrases such as *Allahu Akbar* and *In Shaa Allah*, which often sound intimidating or dangerous to those who do not understand their meaning, but they are actually very common expressions in Arabic that mean "God is Great" "and "God Willing." Due to the media presentation of these terms as ones associated with terrorism, people seem worried when they hear them.

In April 2019, a TV series, *Ramy*, aired in the US. It is about the everyday life of a second-generation Arab-(Egyptian)-Muslim-American who lives in New Jersey and the concerns he endures, whether it is about his girlfriend, Ramadan and fasting, or other daily issues. The *New York Times* published an article about how different the show is than expected and how it appears to present a much-needed portrayal of the American Muslim as a normal, regular American (Deb, 2019). Nothing similar had been presented on screen before. The title of the article published was "*Ramy* Is a Quietly Revolutionary Comedy," and they were correct, the show won a Golden Globes Award in 2020. When receiving the award, Ramy Youssef thanked God for the award, and this did not go unnoticed by the media. The next day *The Express Tribune* posted an article "Ramy Youssef opens Golden Globes speech with '*Allahu Akbar*'" (The Express Tribune, 2020). This was one of the first times that many Americans heard the expression "Allahu Akbar" from a Muslim in a non-negative way. The term has usually been associated with negative, aggressive terrorist scenes on the screen. This is an example of how the language reaches the West, and how there are shy attempts by second generation Americans from the Muslim world to change that.

The Arabic language manifests itself in different communities outside of the Arab World. In a discussion with Arabic non-HLLs in Canada, the topic of Arabic greetings was discussed and how the greeting "*As salaam 'Alaikum*"[7] is seen as a Muslim greeting as it has come to be used by the Muslim communities. It is interesting that the term, which does not necessarily have any direct religious reference, has become regarded as a representation of the Muslim identity. This shows the ties and links between Arabic and Islam to the extent that in the present-day world, Muslim non-Arabs are more and more linguistically aware of their choice of lexicon and use Arabic greetings to speak the same language as their prophet spoke. On the other hand, Arab non-Muslims avoid using such a greeting as it is considered to be religiously charged, even with the lack of direct religious references. It has been noted over the last few years that non-Muslim Arabs have started to avoid using *As Salaam 'Alaikum* and are using other greetings equivalent to "good morning" and "good evening" to avoid using a universal Muslim greeting, or to avoid being identified as Muslims themselves.

3.5.2 Arabic proper names in the West

Names reflect part of the identity of the individual. As such, parents choose carefully when they name their children. Politically, names place people within a particular group. In Malta, the Arabic names that were present in the ninth and tenth century gradually disappeared, and they were no longer present by the thirteenth century (Agius, 1981). Today, with immigrants moving from one country to another, people often feel that they should change or adapt their name to fit in better in their new home once they immigrate.

Bosnia is a country in the Western Balkan Peninsula where the majority of the population is Muslim, yet they speak Bosnian, not Arabic. As Virkkula explains, the Muslim majority in Bosnia select Arabic or Muslim names for their children – often with a native sound change (giving them vowel, consonant, accent, and morphological adaptations) (2012). It is interesting that they choose the Arabic variety of the name, not the Christian, when there are two pronunciations or spellings for the name. Muslim names make the person recognizable in a crowd and it is a custom to choose a name that is not used by the Catholic or Orthodox communities, as they want to keep their identity. Names like Abdullah might appear in every generation in a family, which is a very common Muslim name all over the Muslim World. Unlike other Muslim parts of the world, the name Mohamed does not appear a lot because the Muslim-Bosnians believe that with the name of the prophet comes a lot of responsibility to keep up with the positive attributes that the name carries (Virkkula, 2012). Their choice of Muslim names is a means to reflect their identity and to connect and join themselves with the larger Muslim community as a whole, especially after the war which made them hold on to their Muslim identity even more (Virkkula, 2012).

Arabic is a language that is spread out across the world, a language that has native speakers as well second language users all over the globe. The significance of the language and the extent to which it is used are what Chapters 2 and 3 set out to present. The goal is to show the wide presence of the language which, in turn, is reflected in teaching the language outside the Arab World to both the HLL and non-HLL of Arabic. The Arabic language is a language that has maintained its written, classical form for over 1,500 years. It has developed dialects and has been used and then abandoned by certain speakers (Andalusia, Sicily). Its vocabulary (as well as its morphology at times) has been borrowed, adapted, and used by other languages in Africa, Asia, and Europe. Part 2 of this book looks at the practical aspect of teaching Arabic to HLL – including the heritage speakers and the cultural heritage users, i.e. Muslim users, of the language.

Notes

1 Arabic for the person who calls to prayer from the top of the minaret.
2 Arabic for courthouse or tribunal.
3 Haj is the pilgrimage required once in a lifetime of all Muslims who are capable of the journey to Mecca.
4 One of the oldest religious learning institutes founded in 970 and is regarded as one of the leading sources of religious knowledge in the world.
5 The Canadian Arab Institute is a non-profit organization that works on establishing a dialogue about the life and contributions of Canadian Arabs http://www.canadianarabinstitute.org.
6 US and World Population Clock https://www.census.gov/popclock/ retrieved May 2019.
7 Literally means "Peace upon/on you."

Bibliography

Agius, D. A. (1981). A Semitic Maltese inventory with a possible Siculo-Arabic intervention. *Zeitschrift für Arabische Linguistik, 6*, 7–15.

Arab American Institute. (2019, October 15). *Demographics*. Retrieved from Arab American Institute Website https://www.aaiusa.org/demographics.

Berkley Center for Religion. (2019). Peace and world. *Berkley Center for Religion, Peace and World Affairs*. Retrieved from Georgetown University https://berkleycenter.georgetown.edu/essays/demographics-of-islam.

Buckham, J. (1892). What is culture? *The Journal of Education, 36*((24)899), 395. Retrieved from http://www.jstor.org/stable/44037407.

Byrd, D. (2017). *Islam in a post-secular society: Religion, secularity and the antagonism of recalcitrant faith* (pp. 90–134). Leiden; Boston, MA: Brill. Retrieved October 15, 2019, from www.jstor.org/stable/10.1163/j.ctt1w8h30m

Cumoletti, M., and Batalova, J. (2018). *Middle Eastern and North African immigrants in the United States*. Retrieved February 2019, from https://www.migrationpolicy.org/article/middle-eastern-and-north-african-immigrants-united-states.

Dajani, G. (2014, June). *Canadian Arab institute. Institut Canado-Arabe*. Retrieved October 2019, from Canadian Arab Institute. Institut Canado-Arabe http://www.canadianarabinstitute.org/publications/reports/750925-canadians-hail-arab-lands/.

Deb, S. (2019, April 18). Ramy *is a quietly revolutionary comedy*. Retrieved from The New York Times https://nyti.ms/2DwkXgP.

Fargues, P. (2013). International migration and the nation state in Arab countries. *Middle East Law and Governance, 5*(1–2), 5–35. doi:10.1163/18763375-00501001.

Fellman, J. (1982). Maltese, a unique Arabic dialect. *Anthropologie and Santé, 77*(5/6), 896–897.

Gouvernement du Québec. (2019, December 1). *Charter of the French language*. Retrieved December 2019, from http://www.legisquebec.gouv.qc.ca/en/showdoc/cs/C-11.

Granbery, J. (1929). What is culture? *Social Science, 4*(2), 243–244. Retrieved from http://www.jstor.org/stable/23902726.

Houben, V. J. (2003). Southeast Asia and Islam. *The Annals of the American Academy of Political and Social Science, 588*(1), 149–170. Retrieved from http://www.jstor.org/stable/1049859.

Hunwick, J. (1997). The Arabic literary tradition of Nigeria. *Research in African Literatures, 28*(3), 210–223. Retrieved from http://www.jstor.org.lib-ezproxy.concordia.ca/stable/3821003.

MacDonald, J. (1991). What is culture. *The Journal of Museum Education, 16*(1), 9–12. Retrieved from http://www.jstor.org/stable/40478873.

Milman, O. (2016, April 16). *Southwest Airlines draws outrage over man removed for speaking Arabic*. Retrieved from The Guardian https://www.theguardian.com/us-news/2016/apr/16/southwest-airlines-man-removed-flight-arabic.

Nielsen, H. L. (2017). "Arabic-as-Resource" or "Arabic-as-problem"? Arab Heritage learners in Danish postsecondary education. In O. Kagan, M. Carreira and C. H. Chik (Eds.), *The Routledge handbook of heritage language education from innovation to program building [VitalSource Bookshelf version]* (pp. 363–378). New York: Routledge Taylor Francis Group. Retrieved from vbk://9781317541523.

Onireti, I. L., and Abubakar, I. A. (2012). Arabic language and culture in Nigeria. *The Journey So Far, 58*, 88–92. doi:10.7763/IPEDR. 2012. V58. 20.

Popovic, A., and Rashid, A. (1997). The Muslim culture in the Balkans. *Islamic Studies, 2/3 Special issue Islam in the Balkans* (Summer/Autumn), 177–190. Retrieved from https://www.jstor.org/stable/23076193.

Ram, P. (1997). Culture and religion. *Economic and Political Weekly, 32*(7), 310–310. Retrieved from http://www.jstor.org.lib-ezproxy.concordia.ca/stable/4405077.

Statistics Canada. (2012, October). *Statistics Canada*. Retrieved 2018, from linguistic characteristics of Canadians https://www12.statcan.gc.ca/census-recensement/2011/as-sa/98-314-x/98-314-x2011001-eng.cfm.

The Express Tribune. (2020, January 6). *Ramy Youssef opens golden globes speech with 'Allahu Akbar*. Retrieved from The Express Tribune https://tribune.com.pk/story/2132247/4-ramy-youssef-opens-golden-globes-speech-allahu-akbar/andfbclid=IwAR24pj9PX6IKr7Fl0hjz3PPpwzXQhfU0w31ZDXdbbQ_nQUjtIhEe6YWSC7U/.

United Nations, D. o. (2019). *World population prospects 2019 highlights (ST/ESA/SER.A/423)*. New York: United Nations.

Van Dam, N. (2010). Arabic loanwords in Indonesian revisited. *Bijdragen tot de Taal-, Land- en Volkenkunde, 166*(2/3), 218–243. JSTOR. Retrieved from www.jstor.org/stable/27868577.

Venkatraman, C. (2015, April 2). *Swahili: More than just a language*. Retrieved January 2019, from Berkley Center for Religion, Peace and World Affairs, Georgetown University https://berkleycenter.georgetown.edu/posts/swahili-more-than-just-a-language.

Versteegh, K. (2001). Linguistic contacts between Arabic and other languages. *Arabica, 48*(4), 470–508. Retrieved from http://www.jstor.org/stable/4057668.

Virkkula, J. (2012). Muslim names the Bosnian way. *Jouko and Wahlström, Max eds in Balkan Encounters – Old and New Identities In South-Eastern Europe Slavica Helsingiensia, 41*, 153–168. Retrieved from http://www.helsinki.fi/slavicahelsingiensia/preview/sh41/pdf/7.pdf.

Wexler, P. (1980). Problems in monitoring the diffusion of Arabic into West and Central African languages. *Zeitschrift der Deutschen Morgenländischen Gesellschaft, 130*(3), 522–556.

Additional References

Abd-Allah, U. (2006). Islam and the cultural imperative. *CrossCurrents, 56*(3), 357–375. Retrieved from http://www.jstor.org.lib-ezproxy.concordia.ca/stable/24461405.

Ali, A. (2009). High frequency phatic utterances in Arabic: An example of religion-loaded phatic communication. *Zeitschrift für Arabische Linguistik, 50,* 22–38.

Asatrian, Mushegh (2006). Iranian elements in Arabic: The state of research. *Iran and the Caucasus, 10*(1), 87–106.

Brenner, L., and Last, M. (1985). The role of language in West African Islam. *Africa: The Journal of the International African Institute, 55*(4), 432–446. Retrieved from http://www.jstor.org.lib-ezproxy.concordia.ca/stable/1160176.

Casiño, E. (1972). Integration and the Muslim Filipinos. *Philippine Sociological Review, 20*(4), 360–362. Retrieved from http://www.jstor.org/stable/23892185.

Chejne, A. (1965). Arabic: Its significance and place in Arab-Muslim society. *Middle East Journal, 19*(4), 447–470. Retrieved from http://www.jstor.org/stable/4323917.

Chen, X., and Kerr, K. (2014). In pictures: Allah in China. *Contexts, 13*(1), 62–69. Retrieved from http://www.jstor.org.lib.

Dhahir, O. (2015). Studying Arabic as an additional language together with Arab heritage language learners: The intercultural aspects of sociocultural-interactive strategies. *Al-'Arabiyya, 48,* 43–59. Retrieved from http://www.jstor.org/stable/44654038.

Haron, M. (2003). A portrait of the Arabic script at the Cape. *Sudanic Africa, 14,* 33–54.

Karasik, T., and Benard, C. (2004). Muslim diasporas and networks. In A. Rabasa., C. Benard, P. Chalk, C. Fair, T. Karasik, R. Lal, I.O. Lesser, D.E. Thaler. *The Muslim world after 9/11* (pp. 433–478). RAND Corporation. Retrieved from https://www.rand.org/content/dam/rand/pubs/monographs/2004/RAND_MG246.pdf

Mukhtar, M. (1987). Arabic sources on Somalia. *History in Africa, 14,* 141–172. doi:10.2307/3171836.

Rahman, T. (2000). The teaching of Arabic to the Muslims of South Asia. *Islamic Studies, 39*(3), 399–443.

Razvi, M. (1987). Muslim ummah: Problems and prospects. *Pakistan Horizon, 40*(3), 46–45.

Sanjakdar, F. (2011). Chapter 1: Living Islam in the West. *Counterpoints, 364,* 22–46.

Van der Kroef, J. (1953). The Arabs in Indonesia. *Middle East Journal, 7*(3), 300–323.

Weryho, J. (1986). What is Islamic literature? A book selector's dilemma. *MELA Notes, 37,* 18–24.

Part 2
Heritage language learning pedagogy

This part of the book is the applied, practical part. The focus is on Arabic language learning, the learner, and the classroom. The last three decades have seen an increase in the demand for learning Arabic. There has been a change in both the number of learners and the type of learners, and this has brought about a change in the teaching and the material used. This is what Part 2 of the book looks at: the practical in-class experience of language, both in the Arab World and in North America. Chapter 4 looks at placement and assessment of the HLL, Chapter 5 at the HLL of Arabic within the university educational system, and Chapter 6 examines teaching in the classroom.

4 Heritage language learners and assessment of Arabic language proficiency

4.0 Introduction

This chapter looks at language assessment, mainly at how the language proficiency of a language learner is measured. It also looks at language placement as a formative diagnostic tool that is used to group students of the same level in the same class. Assessment is part of the process that all language learners go through, and HLLs form a distinctive group of these learners. The proficiency tests that are most commonly used for measuring proficiency in Arabic are presented. The assessment of the HLL of Arabic is part of the assessment of ALL, and although what is available at the moment is a good starting point, the road is long and work on placement and assessment in the field of Arabic as a foreign language is needed.

This chapter presents an overview of two standard general methods of measuring proficiency in Arabic. This is important as establishing proficiency levels provides the language learner with the confirmation of where they are when it comes to the language they are learning. It is a tool to say to the learner you achieved this language level because you can fulfill the following tasks. The first proficiency test presented here is based on the American Council of Teaching Foreign Languages (ACTFL) standards and is used mainly in North America. The second, the Common European Framework of Reference for Languages (CEFR), is developed by the Council of Europe and is widely used in Europe. In this chapter, how these two test formats developed over time is outlined, and a brief look at other tests that are used is given. The ACTFL and the CEFR can be seen as the most reliable Arabic language proficiency tests at the moment, with high numbers of language learners taking their tests both in North America and in Europe.

4.1 Standard proficiency tests

Standard proficiency tests measure the language proficiency (oral and or written) of the learner. Learners who have previous knowledge of Arabic need a placement test to measure their language proficiency; this applies to all language learners who come to class with previous knowledge of the language. It is directly related to HLLs as placement is for non-beginners and many of the HLLs are non-beginners. The HLL has basic vocabulary. Usually, this is in dialect, and they are usually familiar with the sounds of the language, and as such their listening skills are above the beginner level. The learner often has a self-assessment and evaluates their own language level. At times, they consider their language skill to be minimal and want to join the beginner level class; at other times, they realize they are not beginners and as such place themselves as intermediate. The language coordinator at the university program can also have oral placement interviews as an assessment; these interviews are not standard, and the results will vary from one assessor to another. Placement tests require more attention from researchers, especially the placement of the HLL of Arabic as the two varieties of Arabic MSA and dialect can play a role in the level of the HLL. Little research has been done on placement of heritage learners, especially false beginners, beginners, and fake beginners.

The need for assessment to measure the proficiency level is a tool used in all fields of learning, and languages are no exception. The English language is the most widely used language in academia in the West and standardized tests for measuring English language proficiency of non-native English speakers have been used for decades. Tests are required by universities for admissions for international students, for immigration applicants, for job purposes, and for different academic and professional purposes. The two most widely used English language proficiency tests are: The International English Language Testing System (IELTS) and the Test of English as a Foreign Language (TOEFL). Both of these tests are designed to measure the English language proficiency of non-English speaking people, for general and academic purposes. The two tests might differ in the format and the scoring system, but the measurement of the language proficiency is reliable and hundreds of thousands of establishments recognize the results of both of these tests. These tests measure all four language skills in separate parts and the final grade for each section is separate as well as a total overall grade.

There is a need for an Arabic language standardized proficiency test, similar to the IELTS and the TOEFL. Currently, there is no single accepted international proficiency test designed to measure the Arabic proficiency of non-Arabic speaking people. There are proficiency guidelines and criteria to measure the level of proficiency that can be applied to any language. The main guidelines that are followed in the West when it comes to measuring proficiency in the Arabic language have been developed by the American Council of Teaching Foreign Languages (ACTFL) and by the Council of Europe, which has developed the Common European Framework of Reference (CEFR). Both ACTFL and CEFR establish guidelines for different languages and Arabic is one of these languages.

4.2 American Council of Teaching Foreign Languages

The American Council on the Teaching of Foreign Languages was founded in 1967 and as its name shows, it does not focus on one language. ACTFL has been working on developing tests across three different organizations. It started when the American Council on Education, the Carnegie Foundation for the Advancement of Teaching, and the College Entrance Examination Board came together in 1947 to form the Educational Testing Service (ETS). On its webpage ACTFL states that it "is dedicated to the improvement and expansion of the teaching and learning of all languages at all levels of instruction" (ACTFL, n.d.). ACTFL recognizes that even though the guidelines were intended for academic and workplace evaluation, they have come to play a role in the educational process as the courses would be designed taking these guidelines into consideration.

Roger Allen (1989) points out that the first grant to ACTFL to establish the generic guidelines and to establish language specific guidelines was in 1981. In 1982, guidelines for French, Spanish, and German were set. The first regional center for proficiency was established at the University of Pennsylvania in 1983. In 1984, a grant to establish guidelines for Modern Standard Arabic was given to the Arabic faculty at the University of Pennsylvania. The guidelines were published in the Journal of the American Association of Teachers of Arabic (AATA), *Al-'Arabiyya*, in November 1985. The guidelines covered the four skills, but they did not look at the different registers that are expected to be used when using the different skills. This is why they needed to be revised. There have been two revisions to the Arabic guides since then; the first revision for both speaking and writing was done in 1999 and 2001, respectively, and the second revision was done in 2012. Allen (1984) (1987) goes on to explain how the educated Arabic speaker speaks the dialect of their geographical location as well as Modern Standard Arabic (MSA), and as such the guidelines should cover both MSA and the colloquial variety so for speaking and listening both MSA and the dialect are needed. On the other hand, the reader and writer of Arabic will do so in MSA alone and so the guidelines for these skills are only for MSA. An educated Arabic speaker has two varieties, the dialect and MSA, and this user chooses to use the appropriate variety according to the situation.

ACTFL has five levels of proficiency: novice, intermediate, advanced, superior, and distinguished speaker of the language (see Figure 4.1). The novice,

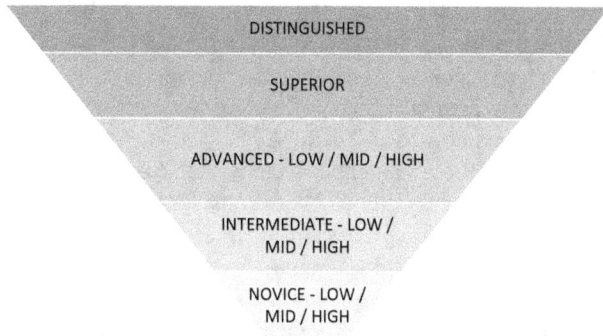

Figure 4.1 ACTFL classification of levels of proficiency of Arabic 2012 guidelines (actfl.org)

intermediate, and advanced levels are divided into subgroups of low, mid, and high. Table 4.1, from the ACTFL Arabic webpage, shows the five levels of proficiency with their subgroups based on the guidelines published in 2012.

Each of the ACTFL levels has a clear set of criteria that the learner needs to achieve correctly to be at that specific level. ACTFL has developed a set of guidelines for proficiency in language instruction and language testing. These guidelines are generic for each proficiency level and apply to all languages. The guidelines apply to Arabic, but specific annotations or adaptations have been added to meet the specific features of the Arabic language. In other words, they have added points to answer the specific features of Arabic. Arabic-specific annotations do not have to be present at every level, as can be seen in the figures: for the writing skill the distinguished and superior levels have annotations while the advanced does not, the generic description applying to Arabic; then the intermediate and the novice have special annotations (ACTFL, 2012b).

As for the Speaking skill, there are special annotations for the Arabic Oral Proficiency Interview (OPI) (see Table 4.2).

This is the speaking component of the ACTFL Proficiency test. It has a scale from 0 to 5, where 5 is the highest. The 2012 Guidelines for Arabic attempt to explain the unique situation of Arabic diglossia:

> ACTFL recognizes that the situation for testing Arabic is a special situation and therefore must be dealt with in a special manner. In the ACTFL test protocol, Arabic is considered to be one language represented by a continuum from all colloquial to all MSA, and a combination of mixes along the continuum.

ACTFL lists the assessment criteria for the different levels, and in the special annotations for the Arabic speaking component there are detailed notes explaining with examples what is language-specific to Arabic. The ACTFL's official webpage states that the OPI "is a standardized procedure for the global assessment of functional speaking ability"; the ACTFL test can be used for both HLLs and non-HLLs. The notes for the speaking skill cover all levels, not like the writing notes. This shows that the Arabic spoken variety needs language-specific notes and the general ACTFL guidelines are not enough. These special annotations give specific, detailed information about how to assess the ALL.

It is important to remember that these guidelines were written for FLL, not for HLLs. This means that they do not necessarily take into consideration the special case of the HLL and the language learning process this learner goes through. It is worth noting that the annotations, at times, give a rationale explaining the criteria of assessment. The rationale can explain more about the culture or the language use in spoken Arabic. For instance, the second point in the distinguished level says, "although Arabic has a vast array of 'cultures,' there are commonalities across the Arabic-speaking world such as the value of the family, role of religion (be it Islam or Christianity), political systems, and a shared literature." This point states a non-language fact about a common cultural point across the Arab World.

Table 4.1 Arabic writing-specific annotations from ACTFL Arabic guidelines (ACTFL, 2012)

Arabic Language Level	*Arabic Specific Annotation*
Distinguished level	A rating of Distinguished is assigned when all the criteria ("tasks, text type, and accuracy") are sustained across a variety of contexts/content areas. In Arabic, this can be accomplished by using MSA and/or vernacular in accordance with contextual requirements of usage.
Superior level	A rating of Superior is assigned when all the criteria ("tasks, text type, and accuracy") are sustained across a variety of contexts/content areas. In Arabic, this can be accomplished by using MSA and/or vernacular in accordance with contextual requirements of usage.
Advanced level (High / Mid / Low)	None.
Intermediate (High / Mid / Low)	None. Time reference need not be present. Basic word order. Time reference need not be present.
Novice High	Shopping lists. Produces short, simple sentences about self, daily life, personal experience. Produces lists, short messages, simple notes, postcards. Uses learned language that is relatively acceptable grammatically. Uses simple connectors to indicate temporal order or addition. Translation from L1 still obvious. Only partially communicates meaning. Letter shape and connecting not yet mastered.
Novice Mid	Mailing address, landing card. Shapes and connects letters successfully. Produces numbers (e.g. four), not numerals (e.g. 4). Provides basic information about self, family members, daily life using learned material Fills in forms (landing card). Provides basic information about self, family members, daily life using learned material Has spelling problems resulting from confusing sounds (long and short vowels, emphatic and non-emphatic etc.). Uses short separate sentences with no specific order. Meaning often depends on learned content words with a limited number of function words. Communicates successfully basic biographical information: name, place of residence. Has serious communication problems beyond formulaic language. Difficult to understand when communicating facts beyond biographical information. Only aware of semantic value of words; not grammatical function. Capable of shaping and connecting letters with relative success using Naskh script.
Novice Low	Only knows the Naskh script. Reproduces learned words and phrases successfully. Produces isolated words and basic information about self (name, nationality, place of residence). Still faces difficulty in shaping and connecting some letters. Spelling problems that result from confusing long and short vowels, emphatic and non-emphatic letters.

Table 4.2 Arabic speaking-specific annotations from ACTFL Arabic guidelines (ACTFL, 2012)

Arabic Language Level	Arabic Specific Annotation
Distinguished level	• At this level of proficiency, cognitive and intellectual maturity as well as the scope and depth of knowledge play an essential part in the ability to speak in a manner typical of Distinguished (e.g. the professional domain, abstract and concrete discussion of a wide variety of topics and use of cultural and literary references). In other words, proficiency is not separate from cognitive and intellectual maturity. • Although Arabic has a vast array of "cultures," there are commonalities across the Arabic-speaking world such as the value of the family, role of religion (be it Islam or Christianity), political systems, and a shared literature. • Sophisticated, coherent discourse is a function of how well read a speaker is. The majority of intellectual topics are acquired from reading in well-respected publications, hence the tendency to use MSA when discussing such topics. • This aspect is especially true of Arabic. A vast proportion of Distinguished speech is dependent of the breadth and depth of reading (and listening, for that matter), which is often written material read out. • There should be a distinction between patterned and sporadic errors. The former almost disappear entirely at the Advanced level. Sporadic, infrequent errors may be expected at the higher levels.
Superior level	• In Arabic, formal and informal settings connote possible use of MSA in the former and possible use of colloquial Arabic in the latter, but not necessarily so. If MSA is the dominant variety, the speaker's speech may be predominantly MSA and vice versa. • Testers should ensure that the discussion is not restricted to topics of personal or special fields of competence. Discussing a variety of topics is the key. Superior speakers should also be able to discuss linguistically unfamiliar topics intelligently. • At this level, the discourse should not only be cohesive (i.e., characterized by the use of cohesive devices), but also coherent where the ideas are logically or chronologically organized. • This is to say that the rate of speech is similar to that of a native speaker. • Using language patterns interchangeably between L1 and L2 is an observed phenomenon, not restricted only to patterns from L1 into L2. • One example is the use by a Superior speaker whose sentence structure in Arabic is more typical of English sentence structure which uses relative clauses where the object pronoun in the dependent clause that refers back to the subject noun in the main clause is dropped. • Low frequency sporadic structural errors include gender and number agreement as well as the use of the wrong imperfect mood of the verb

(*Continued*)

Table 4.2 Continued

Arabic Language Level	Arabic Specific Annotation
Advanced level (High / Mid / Low)	• The ability to sustain performance of Superior-level tasks most of the time may be quantitatively interpreted as 70–80 percent of the time. • The patterns of error that persist up to this level include gender and number agreement as well as the moods of the imperfect. Sometimes, errors in case are also observed. • The ability to discuss topics abstractly in a sustained manner is the hallmark of Superior and Distinguished speakers. • While the use of these communicative strategies reveals the inability to perform consistently at the Superior level, their use at the Advanced level is a sign of solid Advanced performance. • Complex tasks include discussing topics unfamiliar to them, supporting opinion, hypothesizing, and discussing topics abstractly. • At this level, discussing multiple topics is needed in order to ensure the richness and breadth of the vocabulary needed for robust Advanced-level performance. • A linguistic breakdown means the inability to perform the task as expected. • Inadequate performance is different from linguistic breakdown. The output may be correct and to the point, but it is not extensive enough to qualify as a "paragraph." Or the vocabulary may be all right, but not varied enough. • The tasks that can be handled successfully at this level subsume all the global tasks at Advanced and below. • Discussing current events (social, political, local) marks the beginning of a speaker's ability to transcend personal topics and deal with topics of public and general interest. • In Arabic, this point may be equivalent to the control of the moods of the imperfect verb (i.e., the indicative, subjunctive, and jussive). • Advanced Mid speakers may have the feeling that they have full command of the language system, and they flaunt this ability. • This decline is marked by a noticeable increase in errors. • For example, they can describe a program of study, weekend activities at home, and a trip on a holiday.
Intermediate (High / Mid / Low)	• This is the ability to participate in simple dialogues. • Intermediate High speakers can handle Advanced tasks successfully most of the time (i.e., about 70% of the time). • The dominant language manifests itself mainly in sentence structure. • Intermediate speakers should be able to demonstrate ability in asking all kinds of questions, not simply yes/no questions.
Novice (High / Mid / Low)	• Much of the difficulty to understand NM speakers comes from the heavy influence of their L1 phonological system. • This means that they are unable to perform any tasks associated with higher levels.

58 *Heritage language learning pedagogy*

The ACTFL guidelines need updating and the work is not complete. Researchers have noted that ACTFL does not take into consideration the case of diglossia in Arabic; but then it also does not consider varieties of Spanish (Fairclough, 2006) (Son, 2017). In many cases, the HLL is more aware than the non-HLL of the cultural matters and day-to-day living situation in the target language, and this can give the HLL an advantage when it comes to discussing local issues. HLLs can also be quicker in shifting between varieties and this allows them to appear more fluent and to avoid linguistic mistakes they might fall into if it were not for shifting from one variety to another. ACTFL guidelines should take diglossia into account. The special annotations it has for Arabic is a beginning, but more work can be done in this area. Professors of Arabic should be aware of these guidelines and the proficiency levels as this helps them prepare their students to meet the expectations of the proficiency test.

4.3 Common European Framework of Reference for Languages (CEFR)

In Europe, the Common European Framework of Reference for Languages: Learning, Teaching, Assessment (CEFR) was developed as a framework of reference for language learning. It can be used to develop a syllabus, design a course, as well as test students. Similar to ACTFL, the CEFR is not designed for one language but for more than 30 languages – 39 at the moment to be exact. The Council of Europe has translated the CEFR into: Arabic, Albanian, Armenian, Basque, Bulgarian, Catalan, Chinese, Croatian, Czech, Danish, Dutch, English, Esperanto, Estonian, Finnish, French, Galician, Georgian, German, Greek, Hungarian, Italian, Japanese, Korean, Lithuanian, Moldovan, Norwegian, Polish, Portuguese, Russian, Serbian, Slovak, Slovenian, Spanish, Swedish, Turkish, and Ukrainian. As seen from the list, five of these languages are non-European languages – Arabic, Esperanto, Japanese, Korean, and Turkish.

It took more than 20 years to develop the CEFR to the state it has reached today. The concept of establishing a European scheme for second language learning started in the early 1970s. The basic idea was to provide a common foundation to learning a second language, not only with European languages but also eventually with international languages. In the early 1990s, the Council of Europe had reached the point where the recommendation was to use a scale of proficiency levels that could be adopted by any language and that was flexible to work by different languages.

In 2001, the English version of the CEFR was published by Cambridge University Press after it was released by the Council of Europe (Council of Europe, 2001). It is a detailed document, 274 pages, making up nine chapters. The document presents the approach, the levels, the competence of learner/user, the curriculum, and the assessment. The CEFR basically divides proficiency into six broad, global levels, covering the three generally agreed-upon stages of language learning: basic, independent, and proficient. Each of the three levels is divided into two levels as follows: A1 and A2, the basic user; B1 and B2, the independent user; and C1 and C2, the proficient user (see Figure 4.2). Table 4.3, by the Council of Europe, presents the CEFR Language Proficiency Levels.

The CEFR looks at the skill level of the language learner and gives a description of this skill level. The A, B, C levels are equal to a basic, independent, and proficient user of the language, respectively; there is a generic description for each of these levels and it shows the skills the learner can perform. The descriptors are deliberately broad and flexible so that they can be applied on any language, they are not language specific.

From 2001 on, more and more institutions in Europe started using the CEFR as a point of reference to language proficiency. Soliman points out the fact that since 2007 the UK has relied on the CEFR in measuring language proficiency in education (2017). The traditional scales that have been used, such as the Cambridge English exams and the IELTS, align their assessment scales with the CEFR levels to allow comparison. It is safe to say that day after day, it is becoming the standardized proficiency scale for languages used in the UK.

At the moment, there are no clear descriptors of what the A, B, C levels entail, following the CEFR scale specifically for the Arabic language. This means that even though the learners of Arabic at British universities are expected to graduate with a C1 level, we do not have a specific framework for Arabic to determine the competence of the learner. Even with some universities aligning their Arabic courses to the CEFR, this is done per institution and there is a need to develop the scale to meet the Arabic language skills required by each level of proficiency. There have been attempts to develop assessment tests for Arabic based on the CEFR, but they need further development. Soliman (2017) lists some of those attempts and points out that they are mostly based on teacher intuition and that they all focus on MSA only, with the dialect neglected, except for the Al-Arabiyya[1] test, which incorporates some dialect in their assessment.

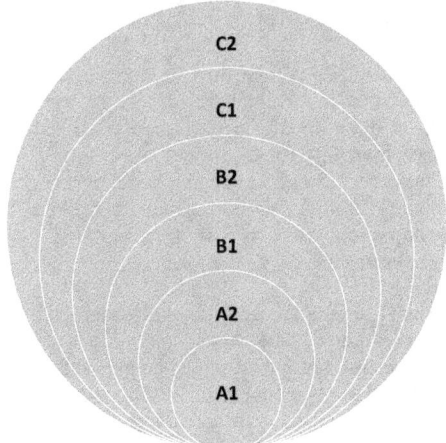

Figure 4.2 CEFR language proficiency levels (Council of Europe Portal, 2019)

Table 4.3 Common reference levels: Global scale (Council of Europe, 2001, p. 24)

Proficient User	C2	Can understand with ease virtually everything heard or read. Can summarize information from different spoken and written sources, reconstructing arguments and accounts in a coherent presentation. Can express him/herself spontaneously, very fluently and precisely, differentiating finer shades of meaning even in more complex situations.
	C1	Can understand a wide range of demanding, longer texts, and recognize implicit meaning. Can express him/herself fluently and spontaneously without much obvious searching for expressions. Can use language flexibly and effectively for social, academic, and professional purposes. Can produce clear, well-structured, detailed text on complex subjects, showing controlled use of organizational patterns, connectors, and cohesive devices.
Independent User	B2	Can understand the main ideas of complex text on both concrete and abstract topics, including technical discussions in their field of specialization. Can interact with a degree of fluency and spontaneity that makes regular interaction with native speakers quite possible without strain for either party. Can produce clear, detailed text on a wide range of subjects and explain a viewpoint on a topical issue giving the advantages and disadvantages of various options.
	B1	Can understand the main points of clear standard input on familiar matters regularly encountered in work, school, leisure, etc. Can deal with most situations likely to arise whilst traveling in an area where the language is spoken. Can produce simple connected text on topics which are familiar or of personal interest. Can describe experiences and events, dreams, hopes, and ambitions and briefly give reasons and explanations for opinions and plans.
Basic User	A2	Can understand sentences and frequently used expressions related to areas of most immediate relevance (e.g. very basic personal and family information, shopping, local geography, employment). Can communicate in simple and routine tasks requiring a simple and direct exchange of information on familiar and routine matters. Can describe in simple terms aspects of their background, immediate environment, and matters in areas of immediate need.
	A1	Can understand and use familiar everyday expressions and very basic phrases aimed at the satisfaction of needs of a concrete type. Can introduce themselves and others and can ask and answer questions about personal details such as where they live, people they know and things they have. Can interact in a simple way provided the other person talks slowly and clearly and is prepared to help.

To conclude, the CEFR is a framework that provides a set of proficiency levels. At the moment, what Arabic language skills the learner needs to master in order to reach each of these levels have not been decided. Yet, the alignment between the CEFR levels and other standardized proficiency tests, such as IELTS and ACTFL, is a step in the right direction.

4.4 Other Arabic proficiency tests

Before moving away from the topic of proficiency testing, it is important to note that neither the ACTFL nor CEFR was the first attempt to design proficiency tests in language learning. There have been smaller-scale summative/proficiency tests used by institutions as long as Arabic has been taught as a foreign language. It is expected that with the current rise in interest in the Arabic language, other standardized tests will be developed specifically for Arabic. Very often language institutes develop their own placement tests. These tests are usually developed by the faculty members and are used as the entrance test when students want to register in an Arabic language course. There are placement tests for students who have previously studied Arabic in other language institutes or learned it in an informal setting at home. The Arabic Language Proficiency Test (ALPT) is a case in point. It was developed in 2002 by The Arab Academy[2] in Cairo. This test follows the ACTFL guidelines and even though it is not global, it has been endorsed by the Islamic Chamber of Commerce and Industry (ICCI) and the Ministry of Religious Affairs in Indonesia (MORA). At the moment, the Arab World Institute in Paris (Institut Du Monde Arabe) has launched an official certificate in the Arabic language. The test has four components covering the four language skills: listening, reading, writing, and speaking. This is a new test that started in May 2019 and was available in eight cities: Paris, Geneva, and six other Arabic cities (Institut du Monde Arabe, 2019). It is based on the CEFR, and there is no feedback on it at the moment. Time will tell how many of the tests currently available will become a standardized test used across the universities and for measuring proficiency.

4.4.1 The Interagency Language Roundtable Test (ILR)

One of the early language tests used on a wide scale was the Interagency Language Roundtable (ILR), it was started by the US government in 1955 (Interagency Language Roundtable, 2011). The rationale for it was to respond to "a need for better coordination and communication in language training and testing among federal agencies." (Herzog, History of the ILR Scale, n.d.). It is an unfunded, federal interagency organization, with no budget to ensure collaboration regarding language learning among different organizations interested in language learning on the federal level. In the early 1950s, the Foreign Service Institute (FSI) with other interested sections of the government formed a committee to develop a single scale to measure a foreign language proficiency. They developed a six-point scale to replace the general terms such as "fluent," "excellent," "very good,"

62 *Heritage language learning pedagogy*

and "good" that were used in official reports. In 1958, the use of an official test in the US to measure language ability in the foreign state became a requirement (Herzog, History of the ILR Scale, n.d.).

The ILR is a scale for federal government employees, even though it did not distinguish between proficiency in the four language skills. This was revised and an FSI Testing Unit was established. Realizing the need to work on separate skills, it designed an oral interview with set criteria to ensure that the results were not subjective. The work of the FSI Testing Unit was recognized world-wide and in 1976 the NATO adopted this language proficiency scale. The revisions continue. The ILR scale now has a 0–5 scale (see Figure 4.3), and there are plus levels included to cover the whole spectrum of language proficiency (Herzog, 2003). The ILR definitions are the basis upon which ACTFL based its work; likewise, other organizations in the US use the ILR scale, with variations to meet their own needs and requirements.

4.4.2 Al-Arabiyya Test

The ILR scale came first, then the ACTFL guidelines and levels were developed. The opposite case, where the guidelines came first then the test, applies to the CEFR guidelines and the Al-Arabiyya test later developed. This is a computer-based test that has been developed by Professor Eckehard Schulz of the Oriental Institute in Leipzig, Germany. The Institute of Oriental Studies was established in 1728 and it appointed its first professor of Arabic at that time (Institute of Oriental Studies, n.d.). In 2011, Professor Schultz established Al-Arabiyya Institute and has since then been working on making the test globally available. The Al-Arabiyya test is based on the CEFR specification to measure levels A2, B1, B2, C1, and C2. The test development started in 2006. It took five years to develop and was available in 2011. This test takes advantage of the modern technology by being computer based and the results are given right after the test. This is another advantage of the eTest. The online sample of the test[3] shows how all levels of the CEFR are available. There are three tests, A1–A2, B1–B2, and

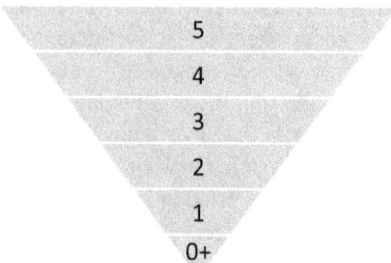

Figure 4.3 The ILR scale (Herzog, History of the ILR Scale)

C1–C2, and for each test they measure the receptive skills, both speaking and reading. It incorporates dialects in the listening section, as well as audio and video questions. The Al-Arabiyya test is an independent test that can be taken anywhere across the globe and they have now added a remote proctor solution to allow tests to be administered anywhere.

4.5 Proficiency tests and the heritage language learner

When it comes to assessment and evaluation of HLLs, there is a noticeable gap in literature. As Son (2017) notes, the little research that has been done in this subfield focused more on the K–12 HLLs and less attention has been given to postsecondary and adult HLLs. He also points out that the research done in this subfield has more often focused on psycholinguistics, phonology, and comparative morphology and syntax learner strategies, with very little attention given to assessment and evaluation.

Proficiency tests are usually taken at the end of the course, but they can be taken at any point while learning a language as they show where the learner is on a specific scale. Proficiency tests are usually a summative evaluation that sum up what the learner knows. The five levels of proficiency of the ACTFL cover the four skills. The goal of every language professor is to have all the language learners at the ACTFL superior level (or CEFR proficient or other equivalent) in all four skills. Realistically, this is not always the case. It is not even possible to say that all HLLs can get to the superior level because there are various factors that play a role in the proficiency level the HLL reaches. Some of these factors are personal, others are academic or even situational.

Al-Batal and Sypher (2007) researched the question of what makes a Superior-level speaker of Arabic. They collected information about students at the Center for Arabic Study Abroad (CASA)[4] who reached the Superior level on the OPI after one year of Arabic. They looked at all the students who completed a one-year study abroad at CASA from 2002 to 2006; this meant looking at 100 fellows. They considered factors that can play a role in the acceptance of the student into this respected program. In addition to the score they get on the tests, the first factor they considered was heritage learners. They also looked at the graduate and undergraduate level, previous living in an Arabic-speaking country (for non-HLLs), proficiency in other languages, and the number of hours studying Arabic. They followed the same view that Husseinali (2006) followed, where the HLLs include those of Arab descent and non-Arab Muslims. Both groups have a connection to the language, even if the proficiency level is not the same at the beginning. This connection with the language is what Valdes (2001) believes is the heritage component, not the level or proficiency of the learner (see Section 5.2).

Out of the 100 Superior level students in the study by Al-Batal and Sypher (Al-Batal & Sypher, 2007), 22 were HLLs and were subdivided: 12 born to Arabic speaking parents, 6 born into Muslim families and had some religious instruction in Arabic, and 4 were Muslim converts who did some studies in Arabic before joining CASA. It is interesting that the study put the 4 converts with the

64 *Heritage language learning pedagogy*

HLL group, but this could be because they wanted to belong to the group and their motivation was personal; they had a personal element that made them appear closer to the HLL group than the regular non-HLL. Their entrance proficiency level could have been relatively higher that the non-HLLs'. What is of interest here is that at the end of the year, 22 of the 100 fellows were HLL. Although the total number of HLLs who studied in the CASA program throughout these four years is not known, it can be assumed that there were more than the 22 that reached Superior level on the OPI. One can ask if there is a way to have more HLLs attain Superior level, and whether or not the heritage factor plays a role in achieving a higher level of proficiency. It also means that after one year in Cairo, not all HLLs necessarily reach the Superior language proficiency.

One point of interest here is that the first factor this study considers when looking at students' proficiency is heritage or non-heritage. The emphasis on this factor brings to mind the question whether the proficiency test should consider this factor and perhaps even have a different test or, at least, scale for the HLL. This is one question that has to be considered when looking at the ACTFL guidelines and if they apply to both the HLL and non-HLL. This is a topic for future research; here the focus is on sharing the current tools used to assess the proficiency of HLLs, and at the moment, the assessment does not distinguish between HLLs and non-HLLs.

4.6 Language placement and the heritage language learner

Standard proficiency tests are used both as a summative test or a formative test. As a summative test, it is at the end of the course to measure what the learners have learned. As a formative assessment, it has the purpose of providing specific feedback to instructors, learners, curriculum developers, and other stakeholders. It can be administered at different stages of instruction in order to track learner development over time (Norris, 2009, p. 587). Proficiency tests usually reflect the communicative level the learner is at as opposed to formative evaluations that measure the current level of the learner. The formative evaluation measures the specific points the learner has reached at specific points during the course, at the beginning, middle, or end of the course. Formative tests are more frequent and are diagnostic in nature and their design is usually different than that of a proficiency test. Formative tests measure specific points that have been taught and are also a guide to what needs to be taught.

For an HLL, establishing the proficiency level and placement starts from the moment they decide to learn their HL. HLLs do not have zero knowledge of the language, even if they believe that they do. This means that most, if not all, of the HLLs need a placement test before they join an adult language course. If studies regarding assessment of HLLs are limited, then studies regarding assessment of HLLs of Arabic are a rarity. Son goes over eight studies on design and implementation of placement tests for HLLs, seven of them are about Spanish as a HL and one on Korean (2017). Out of the eight studies, two studies report the use of a questionnaire with the placement and one reports using a survey of 14 yes/no questions, while five do not mention the use of any other instruments for placement.

The Arabic language is being taught on a larger level than it ever has been before in the West. Still, the numbers of learners of Arabic is far less than the learners of other languages. In case of the HLL of Arabic, there is no established system for placement at the university level. The first evaluation starts with the decision to place the student in the language class that matches their level of Arabic. When a heritage student registers for a class, very often they cannot place themselves correctly. It has been reported that HLLs can feel embarrassed to acknowledge they do not know the HL. There is also diglossia which makes it difficult for the student to evaluate their proficiency in Arabic, as they can be familiar with the dialect but not MSA. This is why having a placement test as a diagnostic and formative tool, which shows the language level of the HLL, would ensure that the learner is placed in the level that corresponds to their language proficiency. HLLs need to be placed according to their level of both varieties of Arabic: dialect and MSA. There are also the M-HLLs who often know how to read the script and understand basic words that they have learned within a religious context but do not speak an Arabic dialect. They can also be familiar with the phonology and sounds of the language.

Depending of the size of the language program and other practical, non-pedagogical matters, choices have to be made. There are decisions that have to be made to ensure the smooth running of a language program. For instance, the program has to make decisions regarding the placement of HLLs, the levels of Arabic language classes it offers, and the language varieties (MSA or dialect) it offers. In a growing program at an established university in Canada, the program offers MSA (no Arabic dialect) and it starts from the total beginner level. A placement test is available online for all these languages so that a learner with previous knowledge of the language has to take the placement test.

As Arabic does not use the Latin script, but uses the Arabic script, this is one of the first problems HLLs face. They can speak the language but not read or write it. This means that an HLL of Arabic can register in the beginner class and they are not wrong in doing so; they actually do not read and write and as such are beginners. To overcome this issue a note was added to the placement test saying that if you are an HLL of Arabic but cannot read or write, you need to contact the department and have an oral assessment for your placement. This oral interview measures the same items as the written placement test: morphology, grammar, and comprehension to assess which level of Arabic the learner would be placed in if they could read and write. If the HLL has minimal knowledge of Arabic, then they would be placed in an accelerated beginner class where the script is taught but in a shorter time than the non-HLL class. If the HLL is an advanced speaker of the language, then the ideal solution is to have a short intensive course of basic writing, starting with the alphabet, given over a limited number of hours. Then the learner can join the intermediate or advanced language class. If in a small program this is not possible (see Sections 6.1 and 6.4), but the oral placement has revealed that this learner cannot join the beginner classes because of their higher knowledge of vocabulary and grammar, then the learner should not be permitted to take the Arabic language class.

Again, practical questions have to be considered. These include availability of qualified language professors to conduct the oral interviews for placement purposes as well as availability of a budget to open separate language classes for HLLs and non-HLLs at the initial, beginner level. Thus, a language institution has to consider the placement system it is going to use according to the resources available to it. The placement can be one or more of the following: a questionnaire, a written multiple-choice test, an open-ended essay/written test, a listening test, an interview, or a combination of one or more of these placement tools.

Notes

1 Al-Arabiyya Institute was founded in 2011 by Professor Schulz of the Oriental Institute, University of Leibzig, https://toafl.com/about-us.
2 Arab Academy offers a large number of Arabic online courses and has its own proficiency test that it says has been recognized by international universities, www.arabacademy.com.
3 Al-Arabiyya Free Online Arabic Test, https://toafl.com/sample-tests
4 CASA is a consortium of 28 American universities that provides intensive advanced-level training leading to Superior level proficiency in Arabic language and culture. CASA offers advanced level training in Arabic language and culture to qualified American students at The American University in Cairo and Qasid Arabic Institute in Amman. See https://casa.fas.harvard.edu/program-main-page

Bibliography

ACTFL. (2012a). *ACTFL proficiency guidelines speaking*. Retrieved from https://www.actfl.org/publications/guidelines-and-manuals/actfl-proficiency-guidelines-2012/arabic/arabic-consensus-project/speaking.
ACTFL. (2012b). *ACTFL proficiency guidelines writing*. Retrieved from https://www.actfl.org/publications/guidelines-and-manuals/actfl-proficiency-guidelines-2012/arabic/arabic-consensus-project/writing.
ACTFL. (n.d.). *ACTFL*. Retrieved from https://www.actfl.org/about-the-american-council-the-teaching-foreign-languages.
Al-Batal, M., & Sypher, C. (2007). Toward superior-level proficiency in Arabic: A study of successful casa full-year applicants 2002–2006. *Al-'Arabiyya*, *40/41*, 57–70. Retrieved from http://www.jstor.org.lib-ezproxy.concordia.ca/stable/43195686.
Allen, R. (1984). The ACTFL guidelines and Arabic. *Al-'Arabiyya*, *20*(1/2), 43–49. Retrieved from http://www.jstor.org/stable/43191687.
Allen, R. (1987). The ACTFL guidelines and Arabic. *Al-'Arabiyya*, *20*, 43–50.
Allen, R. (1989). Arabic proficiency guidelines. *Foreign Language Annals*, *22*(4), 373–392.
Council of Europe. (2001). *Council of Europe*. Retrieved from Council of Europe portal www.coe.int/en/web/common-european-framework-reference-languages/level-descriptions.

Council of Europe Portal. (2019). *Common European framework of reference for languages CEFR*. Retrieved March 2019, from Council of Europe Portal https://www.coe.int/en/web/common-european-framework-reference-languages/level-descriptions.
Fairclough, M. (2006). Language placement exams for heritage speakers of Spanish: Learning from students' mistakes. *Foreign Language Annals, 39*(4), 595–604.
Herzog, M. (2003). Impact of the proficiency scale and the oral proficiency interview on the foreign language program at the Defense Language Institute Foreign Language Center. *Foreign Language Annals, 36*(4), 566–571. doi:10.1111/j.1944-9720.2003.tb02146.x.
Herzog, M. (n.d.). *History of the ILR scale*. Retrieved from Interagency Language Roundtable (ILR) https://www.govtilr.org/Skills/IRL%20Scale%20History.htm.
Husseinali, G. (2006). Who is studying Arabic and why? A survey of Arabic students' orientations at a major university. *Foreign Language Annals, 39*(3), 395–412.
Institut du Monde Arabe. (2019). www.imarabe.org. Retrieved from https://www.imarabe.org/fr/actualites/centre-de-langue-et-de-civilisation-arabes/2019/certification-en-arabe-inscrivez-vous-a.
Institute of Oriental Studies. (n.d.). Retrieved from Orientalisches Institut Universität Leipzig https://www.orient.uni-leipzig.de/institute/struktur/arabische-sprach-und-ubersetzungswissenschaft/?L=1.
Interagency Language Roundtable. (2011). Retrieved from https://www.govtilr.org.
Soliman, R. (2017). The implementation of the common European framework of reference for the teaching and learning of Arabic as a second language in higher education. In K. M. Wahba, L. England & Z. Taha (Eds.), *Handbook for Arabic language teaching professionals in the 21st century, volume 2* (pp. 118–140). Mahwah, NJ: Lawrence Erlbaum.
Son, Y. (2017). Toward useful assessment and evaluation of heritage language learning. *Foreign Language Annals, 50*(2), 367–386. doi:10.1111/flan.12273.
Valdes, G. (2001). Heritage language students: Profiles and possibilities. In J. Peyton & D. K. Ranard, & McGinnis (Eds.), *Heritage languages in America: Preserving a national resource* (pp. 37–80). Washington D.C. and McHenry, IL: The Center for Applied Linguistics and Delta Systems.

Additional References

Allen, R. (1987). "Arabic proficiency guidelines," & "The Arabic guidelines: Where now?" In C. W. Stansfield & W. Chip Herman (Eds.), *ACTFL Proficiency Guidelines for the less commonly taught languages*. Washington D.C: Center for Applied Linguistics.
Allen, R., & Allen, R. (1987). The ACTFL guidelines and Arabic. *Al-'Arabiyya, 20*(1/2), 43–49.
Alnassan, A. (2017). L'enseignement de l'arabe L2 entre l'héritage et la nouveauté en didactique des langues vivantes. *Bellaterra Journal of Teaching and Learning Language and Literature, 10*(1), 20–41. doi:10.5565/rev/jtl3.665.
Fox, E. (2019). A new certificate measures Arabic language proficiency. Retrieved from https://www.al-fanarmedia.org/2019/05/a-new-certificate-measures-arabic-language-proficiency/ Alfanar Media Covering Education, Research and Culture 20 May 2019.
Hammoud, S. (1996). A survey of current classroom practices among teachers of Arabic. *Al-'Arabiyya, 29*, 95–128.
Heath, P. (1990). Proficiency in Arabic language learning: Some reflections on basic goals. *Al-'Arabiyya, 23*(1/2), 31–48.

Martin, C. (2010). Assessing the oral proficiency of adult learners, "heritage" and "native" speakers using the "ILR descriptions" and "ACTFL proficiency guidelines": Considering the challenges. *Russian Language Journal / Русский язык, 60*, 167–181.

Norris, J. M. (2009). Task-based teaching and testing. In M. H. Long & C. J. Doughty (Eds.), *The handbook of language teaching* (pp. 578–594). Malden, MA: Wiley-Blackwell.

Parkinson, D. (1987). Introduction to pedagogy section. *Al-'Arabiyya, 20*(1/2), 9–11.

Taha, Z. (2007). Educated spoken Arabic: How could it help in redefining the ACTFL guidelines? *Al-'Arabiyya, 40/41*, 104–114.

5 The heritage language learner of Arabic

5.0 Introduction

This chapter looks at the learners of Arabic in North America and Europe. It looks more closely at the HLLs of Arabic. Today, the second generation (and often third generation) of Arab immigrants is showing a more noticeable interest in learning the language of their parents and family. Also, Muslim immigrants are looking at learning the language of their faith. All this has led to a diversity of learner background in the Arabic language classroom, a diversity that was not as obvious in the past as it is today. Yet, not all HLLs are one homogenous group.

The chapter takes a closer look at the HLL and divides this group into two subgroups, the geographical HLL (G-HLL) and the Muslim-heritage language learner (M-HLL),[1] to see where they meet and where they differ. The last section of this chapter presents individual HLLs to understand how students see the Arabic language learning experience and the need to learn it from a heritage, social, and non-academic point of view. The goal here is to understand the HLLs in order to better help them learn the language.

5.1 The language learner of Arabic

Chapter 4 looked at how to measure proficiency of the ALL and also gave an overview of the standardized tests that are used to measure the proficiency of language learners. Chapter 5 starts by briefly identifying the ALL as this is the larger group to which the HLL of Arabic belongs. It starts by looking at the ALL in the US, Canada, and Denmark. The Modern Languages Association[2] (MLA) presents information regarding the most commonly taught languages in the US over more than fifty years (Looney and Lusin, 2018, p. 16). This information gives an idea about which languages are growing and which are not. It allows those in the field to have up-to date data to see what is happening within the teaching of languages in higher education. This allows for Arabic to be seen in comparison to other foreign languages. It is a way to discover the demand today for learning Arabic and to find out if the numbers of learners show significant change over the years, and in which direction the change is.

Table 5.1 presents the MLA data for the top ten languages taught in the US. It shows that Spanish is the most taught language with 712,240 learners enrolled

Table 5.1 Adapted from MLA enrollment survey – 2016 enrollments in the most commonly taught languages in the US institutions of higher education in selected years

	1958	1980	1995	2006	2009	2013	2016
Spanish	126,303	378,952	606,286	822,148	861.015	789,888	712,240
French	157,900	248,303	205,351	206,019	215,244	197,679	175,667
American Sign Language			4,304	79,744	92,068	109,567	107,060
German	107,870	127,015	96,263	94,146	95,613	86,762	80,594
Japanese	844	11,156	44,723	65,410	72,357	66,771	68,810
Italian	9,577	34,793	43,760	78,176	80,322	70,982	56,743
Chinese	615	11,266	26,471	51,382	59,876	61,084	53,069
Arabic	364	3,471	4,444	24,010	35,228	33,526	31,554
Latin		25,019	25,897	32,164	32,446	27,209	24,866
Russian	16,042	23,987	24,729	24,784	26,760	21,979	20,355

in Spanish courses in 2016, followed by French which has 197,667 learners enrolled. This large difference between Spanish and French echoes what was said in Chapter 1, that Spanish is the largest HL in the US. It is no surprise that research in the field of SLA has focused largely on Spanish. A look at German shows that it was among the top languages in 1958, and it had more than 100,000 students, but beginning in 1990 the numbers decreased. In 2016, the number of enrollments for German decreased from 107,870 to 80,594; a change of minus 25.3 percent.

On the other hand, Arabic had only 364 learners in 1958, but had 31,554 learners in 2016, showing a large and noticeable increase of 8,568.7 percent. Table 5.2 below is based on the work of Looney and Lusin (2018, p. 16) and shows the enrollment numbers in Arabic in US higher education.

When looking at the data available on Arabic, the MLA notes that institutions give different names to the Arabic variety they teach; so it "includes enrollments reported under 'Arabic,' 'Arabic, Algerian,' 'Arabic, Classical,' 'Arabic, Egyptian,' 'Arabic, Gulf,' 'Arabic, Iraqi,' 'Arabic, Levantine,' 'Arabic, Modern Standard,' 'Arabic, Moroccan,' 'Arabic, Qur'anic,' 'Arabic, Sudanese,' and 'Arabic, Syrian'" (Looney and Lusin, 2019, p. 88). A look at the status of Arabic in the US reveals that even though Arabic is not one of the top immigrant languages in the US, there has been an increase in the number of immigrants from the Arab World recently.

Table 5.2 Enrollment in Arabic in higher education institutions in the US in selected years.

Year	1958	1970	1980	1990	1995	2002	2006	2009	2013	2016	% Change 1958–2016
Arabic	364	1,333	3,471	3,683	4,444	10,584	24,010	35,228	33,526	31,554	8,568.7

The increase in the number of learners of Arabic is noticeable. As the numbers show, the first major increase in enrollment occurred between 1995 and 2002 and it continued after that. In 1995, the institutions reported 4,444 enrollments in Arabic and 21 years later the numbers are up to 31,554 students, in 2016. This is a seven-fold increase in the number of students learning Arabic. The numbers do not detail students' backgrounds, but it can be assumed that the increase in the number of HLLs has increased, especially since the number of Arab immigrants has been increasing during this last four decades.

The increase in the number of learners of Arabic is seen in Canada as well. Canada is different than the US when it comes to languages, partly because Canada has two official languages, English and French. This is one of the reasons why SLA has received a lot of attention in Canada. Yet, there is no institute in Canada similar in the MLA, and as such, data about learners is not readily available. There is no nation-wide data regarding the number of language learners of Arabic in Canada; there are shy attempts to collect data, but they are on an individual, small-scale basis. The Canadian Association of Second Language Teachers (CASLT)[3] was established in 1970 to discuss issues that are important to the second language teachers, but it does not collect data about the language learners in Canada.

The number of Arab immigrants in Canada has been increasing and it follows that the use of Arabic has seen a noticeable increase. According to Statistics Canada, Arabic is the third largest immigrant language in Canada with speakers reaching 108,000 in Montreal alone in 2011 (Statistics Canada, 2012). With the increase of families speaking Arabic, one can expect an increase in the number of HLLs taking Arabic language classes. As each province has different education and language laws on the school education level, teaching Arabic is not done the same way across Canada. On the official level, it has been taught as an additional, immigrant language at schools in a number of provinces but not necessarily in all of the provinces. In Edmonton, Alberta, there is a bilingual school program and Arabic language is an option together with Chinese (Mandarin), French, German, Hebrew, and Spanish.[4] There are four bilingual English/Arabic schools, one junior high and one senior school in Edmonton. These are government public schools, not private schools like in the other provinces in Canada. The different language policies in Canada compared to the US make for a different language learner, one that has an increased language awareness since their early years.

One way to find out the direction teaching Arabic is taking is to look at numbers of learners in one institute over a number of years. Information about a program in Montreal, Canada can be taken as an example of how the number of learners of Arabic are increasing. In this established Montreal university, Arabic language courses are taught as part of a minor or as an elective. The number of students registered in the language courses has been on a continual and gradual increase from 2015 until the present. In 2015, 113 students registered in the beginner and intermediates classes; in 2017 there were 160 students registered, and in 2019 the number went up to 172 students. This brings the total number to 743 students within four years in one university in Canada. There are 96 universities across Canada, and most of them offer Arabic courses as a language option for their students. This gives an idea about the interest that learning Arabic is receiving in Canada.

The study of language acquisition, bilingualism, and heritage languages is taking place on both sides of the ocean, in North America and in Europe. Yet in order to compare the data, the studies need to have similar settings for both places. A study on HLLs in Denmark or England and a similar HLL study on HLLs in Michigan or Montreal, for example, with similar criteria except for the location, have not been done yet. To date, there are no similar studies, but since the study of heritage languages is still at its beginning, more studies regarding HLLs of Arabic are expected, and maybe a study will look at location to see the difference it has.

Turning to Europe to see where Arabic stands as a HL, it is evident that Denmark is a country that has seen a growth in the number of users of Arabic as well as an interest in learning the language. Denmark is a country with a population of 5.7 million,[5] smaller in population than Canada, and Arabic is the largest non-Western language spoken in Denmark with a little less than 100,000 speakers in the 2015 census (Nielsen, 2017). Arabic-speaking migrants started to arrive in Denmark in smaller numbers in the 1960s, but with the political events that have occurred in the Arab World, there has been a recent increase in the number of Palestinians, followed by Iraqis and, more recently, Syrians. Even though there is no accurate data regarding the number of students of Arabic in Denmark, the data from one study gives an idea about the number of learners studying Arabic at the university level. Dhahir has conducted a study in a university in Denmark and he reports sending questionnaires by email to all the 270 students who took Arabic over five years at one said university in Denmark; he reports that his participants were "motivated to study Arabic by a positive attitude toward other cultures and a particular curiosity to explore Arabic and Islamic culture" (2015, p. 48).

The increase in interest in learning Arabic as a foreign language can be attributed to the increase in the number of Arab immigrants, as well as political and economic reasons. More and more classes are now open at the university level to meet the increase in demand from the learners. At the same time, the number Arabic HLLs registering to attend university classes has also been increasing. The HLLs are not the main reason the classes are being opened, but their presence in the language classroom adds to the class diversity and raises awareness regarding a subgroup of language learners with a different language background than what was more common in earlier years.

5.2 Defining the heritage language learner of Arabic

Having looked at the changes in the numbers of language learners of Arabic in the West, this section looks at the language learners, in particular the HLLs of Arabic. Learners can be grouped according to their relationship with the language. Each individual HLL of Arabic is a mixture of this specific learner's situation and knowledge of the different varieties of the language. A general, more common type of language learner who comes to an Arabic class is presented here. In short, the HLLs of Arabic that are presented here share the following: (1) They are university students who have Arabic or Muslim family names. They can also have an Arabic or Muslim first name, but not necessarily. Many HLLs have Western first names (in case of G-HLL, non-Muslim students, for example), and also often students can have an Arabic or Muslim name without being HLLs (as with many of the American-born African names such as Jamal, Karim, and others). (2) They do not know MSA and are familiar with a dialect, to a certain level of fluency. (3) These learners have either never learned to read or write, or they have started learning but have not continued learning to the proficiency level of native speakers. (4) They can be language learners of a beginner, intermediate, or advanced level. (5) They identify as belonging to the Arabic culture and heritage. (6) They are raised in the West, either born or having moved to the West at a very young age.

Before going further, there are important points to remember. First, a HLL is not the same as a HL speaker; the speaker already knows the language and uses it and does not necessarily go to the language class. The research on SLA and bilingualism looks at heritage speakers is detail. While research in applied linguistics and language learning looks at HLs and HLLs, it does not examine the theories of bilingualism. The heritage speakers who do not become proficient in the HL as children or young teens and come to learn it at the university level become HLLs. However, not every heritage speaker becomes a HLL.

This HLL is a young adult who has made the conscious decision to come to the class to increase their proficiency in a language that they are connected to, through family, faith, or culture. The learner wants to learn the language, and at the same time they are usually concerned that they might be "late," that they should have learned the language earlier. In many cases, there is the sense of guilt or embarrassment hanging over the HLL's head when they cannot master the HL. This is why the support and positive encouragement of the language professor is important, as positive feedback makes the HLL more at ease when learning the HL.

A second important point to note here is that the term "Arabic heritage learners" can be misleading. Arabic is a language, not an ethnicity. The HLL of Arabic is a broader and more accurate term, as the learners are not always Arab by ethnicity; they can be Muslim from anywhere, Iran, Turkey, Pakistan, Indonesia, or China. They share an Arabic heritage, which comes with the religion. On the other hand, they can be from the Arab World geographically, but identify as a different ethnicity, such as Amazigh, Kurd, Nubian, Egyptian, Phoenician, among others. Arabic native speakers from outside the Arabian Peninsula can often belong to an ethnic group that speaks Arabic, especially with the minority groups, such as Amazigh, Kurd, and Nubian. Other HLs do not have this point to consider.

The HLL identified here is a mature student who has finished their school education and has chosen to formally learn Arabic at the university level. This learner is different from a bilingual child learning the language at home. When discussing HLLs, Duff and Li (2009) point out that these learners are not all one homogenous group and that the use of the HL differs from one family to another. There are families that raise the children bilingual, using both the official language and the

HL, and these become heritage speakers without formal learning. At the same time, they point out that,

> In other cases, children and adults ... may have only latent or partial knowledge of the ancestral[6] language, often in a spoken vernacular, without a full range of literacy skills and with limited knowledge of standard varieties of the language or of the varieties taught in formal educational settings; they may not possess a full range of registers in the language, including academic registers and sociolinguistically differentiated language reflecting different levels of formality and politeness.
>
> (Duff and Li, 2009, p. 2)

Even though they are not referring to a specific language or a specific HLL, this applies to a large extent to the HLL of Arabic at the university level. They refer to the vernacular, the literacy, and the different language registers. These are key issues the HLL of Arabic faces: the spoken dialect and diglossia, the Arabic written script, and not possessing all the language registers in MSA.

HLLs of Arabic are different than HLLs of other languages (such as the Spanish for example) in that the HLL of Arabic more than often comes to the beginner Arabic class to learn MSA, due to Arabic diglossia; the HLL can be a good speaker of a dialect but at the same time this HLL has zero knowledge of MSA and the written script. There are language registers that this HLL is not familiar with. Now, there are distinctions between the HLLs of Arabic that need to be made clear, and variations between the HLLs that need to be discussed and analyzed.

5.2.1 Two different subgroups of HLLs of Arabic: G-HLL and M-HLL

In North America, waves of immigration from the Arab World can be seen from the early twentieth century and have continued until the present day (see Section 3.4.1). The Arabic language has traditionally been associated with Islam, and the majority of Arabs are Muslims; but the Arabic HLL is not necessarily Muslim, a noticeable group of Arabic HLLs is non-Muslim (Arab American Institute, 2019). As a matter of fact, the first wave of Arab immigrants to the Americas were the Christians from the Levant area, and the majority of immigrants from Egypt are Egyptian Christian Copts (they form the majority of the immigrants in Montreal, for example). So, the first thing to note about that HLL of Arabic is that they are not necessarily Muslim. This group will be referred to as *Geographical HLL* or G-HLL of Arabic where the family of the G-HLL uses a dialect of Arabic and comes from an Arabic-speaking country.

There is a second group of learners of Arabic that is not only from the Arab World, but is from the Muslim World, and these people share common grounds with the G-HLL to the extent that they are very often considered as part of the HLLs of Arabic. *Muslim-heritage language learners* (M-HLLs) come from countries that do not have Arabic as a mother tongue, but Arabic is a language used in a religious context. These include learners that are from Muslim countries such as Pakistan, Afghanistan, Bangladesh, Iran, and Turkey. In addition, there is also the Muslim learner from Asia, Indonesia, and Malaysia who moved to the West. This appears to be a smaller group of learners in the Arabic class, but a noticeable one, nonetheless. As all Muslims recite the Quran and pray in Arabic and use the language for religious purposes regularly, they can be seen as a special subgroup of HLL. Also, this group can be familiar with the script of Arabic as it is used in their native, mother tongues that the family uses if they speak Persian, Urdu, Azerbaijani, Pashto, or Kurdish. M-HLLs do not speak an Arabic dialect at home nor does their family come from an Arabic-speaking country. Both groups of learners, G-HLL and M-HLL, share large elements of the culture and traditions. Henceforth, the term HLL will be used as an umbrella term for both G-HLL and M-HLL, unless a specific subgroup is intended.

Looking at the HLLs according to their relation to the Arabic language, it can be seen that they come to learn Arabic either for family heritage, like the G-HLL (who might or might not be Muslim), or religious heritage, like the M-HLL. From a language learning perspective, the G-HLL has the dialect at home to give them support in learning MSA, as well as the cultural experience of having an Arabic family. The linguistic skills the G-HLL brings to class do not change because of religious background. Both the Muslim and non-Muslim G-HLL share the knowledge of the culture and the heritage. The M-HLL does not have the dialect at home but is highly motivated to learn the language. To sum it up, the Arabic HLL can be seen to belong to one of two main groups: either Arab G-HLL (Muslim or non-Muslim) or Muslim-heritage language learner (M-HLL), and they are both keen on learning MSA.

For the M-HLL, this learner has basic or minimal knowledge of CA (and at times knows basic MSA). They can read the script if the family originally comes from a country that uses the Arabic script, or if they have been to a religion school as children – which is a common custom for many M-HLL. This group of learners can be seen as "language readers"; they share a Muslim heritage with many of the G-HLL, and this is what distinguishes them from G-HLLs and non-HLLs when they learn Arabic.

The effect of the Arabic language on the vocabulary and morphology of the languages of many Muslim countries cannot go unnoticed (as seen in Section 3.2). For instance, it is said that from 25 to 40 percent of the Persian lexicon is related to Arabic, depending on the genre one is looking at; some sources put this up to 40 to 50 percent due to the influence of Islam (Iranian languages, 2016). Table 5.3 below summarizes how the HLL of Arabic belongs in one of two groups based on the geographical and religious background. It shows how both groups share common factors and how the two groups differ.

One of the main aims of this book is to attempt to describe the subgroups of HLLs of Arabic in order to have a clear understanding of this learner. To understand this learner, it is necessary to know who the learner is and why they learn the language. The definition of the HLL by Valdes is our starting point to define the HLL of Arabic. When he discusses HLL, Valdes says that

Table 5.3 HLL of Arabic by group

		Background	Familiarity with spoken dialect	Familiarity with written language	Reasons for learning Arabic	Religious background	Heritage (culture) knowledge
The HLL of Arabic	Group I Geographic-HLL (G-HLL)	From the Arab World	Family speaks an Arabic dialect	Parents read and understands the Arabic script	Learn Arabic for family and religion	Muslim	Share the Arabic culture, values, traditions
	Group II Muslim-HLL (M-HLL)	Not from Arab World	Family does not speak an Arabic dialect	Parents read the Arabic script (e.g. from Persia)	Learn Arabic for family Learn Arabic for religion	Not Muslim Muslim	Share many of the Arabic culture, values, traditions

the term heritage language has been used broadly to refer to non-societal and non-majority languages spoken by groups often known as linguistic minorities. Those members of linguistic minorities who are concerned about the study, maintenance, and revitalization of their minority languages have been referred to as heritage language students.

(Valdes, 2005, p. 411)

Here, Valdes talks about both: the HL and the HLL who have an interest in "the study, maintenance and revitalization" of the HL. When this basic definition is applied to Arabic, the HL is both forms of Arabic – MSA and the local dialect. This is true for the G-HLL, but for the M-HLL only MSA is the HL they are seeking.

The G-HLL is familiar with the dialect and can communicate using an Arabic dialect to a certain extent (this can vary according to the personal situation). Even though the learner can speak the dialect of his family to a certain extent, the G-HLL may or may not have formally or informally studied MSA – including writing the Arabic script. Based on the above definition by Valdes, the G-HLL of Arabic is coming to class for "the study, maintenance and revitalization" of Arabic – depending on how much Arabic the learner knows. While the M-HLL is coming to *study* the language but not *maintain*, nor *revitalize* it, since their family does not speak a dialect, they are coming to learn a formal variety that enables them to connect to their faith.

As Benmamoun et al. (2013) point out, defining a HLL is not a clear-cut task as not all HLLs are exactly the same, as seen above. This is why when discussing HLLs always start by describing the specific learner and the context of exposure to the HL (which is not necessarily formal learning but can be simply exposure to the dialect variety of the HL). In an attempt to define the heritage speaker, Benmamoun et al. (2013) present a number of defining factors and definitions to show how broad a spectrum the HLL can cover; they include a broad definition where the heritage speaker is a speaker with "ethnic, cultural or other connection with a language, regardless of whether that person learned the heritage language as a child" (Benmamoun, Montrul, and Polinsky, 2013, p. 260). I would add that this connection has to be a permanent connection, not a temporary connection, so the learners relate to the language as a HL. This definition applies to the case of the M-HLL of Arabic as it finds a place for them to be included since they do have a connection with the language even though they are not a *speaker* of the language.

In summary, the HLLs of Arabic are a heterogenous group; they share some aspects and also differ in other aspects. Their language proficiency and their background can differ greatly. The HLL (including both G-HLL and M-HLL) is an individual who decides at a point in their life to formally learn Arabic, the language of their family or of their faith. They have been exposed to this language at a young age to various degrees, but they have not reached a complete mastering of all skills. This learner has knowledge of the culture and the traditions to which the Arabic language belongs. One point to add here, the HLL can be familiar with the Arabic written script or not (unlike HLLs of other languages that use the Latin script and do not have to formally learn a script for the HL class). Often, Muslim learners from countries that use the Arabic script (such as Iran) can write the language, while HLLs from the Arab World cannot.

Before moving on, it is important to point out some basic key information about the classes and the general levels offered at the university level. In a program that offers Arabic language MSA, the beginner courses start teaching the language from the very beginning – they usually start with the writing skill and teaching the alphabet. After that, the course starts introducing vocabulary and grammar; remember it is not like teaching French, Italian, German, or Spanish where the languages use the Latin script similar to the English script. The Arabic beginner class is basic, and this is the point where most of the programs start from when they teach Arabic in the US, Canada, or Europe. When teaching speaking, they usually start with phonemes and the pronunciation of single sounds and move from there.

As for HLLs, they can be beginner, intermediate, or advanced students. The learner who is fluent in the dialect and wants to improve their MSA reading and writing language skill is not discussed here; this learner forms a smaller percentage of HLLs coming to language classes at the university level. The focus here is mainly on the beginner MSA HLL, the largest group of HLLs that register in the Arabic classes. This beginner MSA HLL is expected to progress at higher rates and relatively quickly once they learn how to read and write, and they will need to be in a separate intensive class. In larger programs (there is a small group of such programs at the moment) they would be in a separate MSA reading and writing class. Our concern here is the learner is learning Arabic for the first time in a formal learning setting, like most of the HLLs that come to the university class. This HLL does not have full command of the HL and they do not have high proficiency in all the language skills. They do, on the other hand, have an overall understanding of the context and culture of Arabic. They usually know how the Arabic culture differs from, or agrees with, Western culture in certain cultural aspects. Thus, both the G-HLL and the M-HLL come to class with linguistic and cultural tools that the non-HLL does not have.

It is important to remember that the G-HLL is aware of diglossia and, to some extent, so is the M-HLL; each one of them is more familiar with and acquainted to a different form of the language: MSA or dialect. All native Arabic speakers are exposed to more than one variety. They use two different language varieties according to the purpose of the interaction or the situation; this is diglossia for the Arabic speaker. It is safe to say that every Arabic native speaker learns MSA, as it is a taught variety of the language. This can be done at school or even by listening to the religious recitals that are mostly in CA. HLLs are taught a formal variety when they are taught to pray, whether they are Muslim or Christian (although less Arabic is used in Arabic churches in the West today). The HLL comes to class with this understanding: they are aware that they do not speak MSA form before ever registering for a class. This language awareness is present for the HLL, but not necessarily for the non-HLL.

5.3 Family and the heritage language learner

Researchers in SLA have always looked at the family and its role in developing the second language. Research has usually looked at bilingual children and the language policy that the family chooses to follow to bring up a bilingual individual starting from childhood. Yet, when it comes to the family and HLLs at the university level, little research is done to examine whether or not the family influences the HLL. HL (and HLLs) is a more recent area of study in SLA and this is the reason why little research on the role of the family has been done. Also, it might not be clear yet how to study the role of the family when the HLL is an adult, and it is very different than studying language acquisition of children in bilingual families. What is known is that the HLL of Arabic is not a proficient bilingual speaker of English and Arabic, and the family language policy in their home as a child did not allow them to become a fluent bilingual.

A general consensus among language professors of Arabic is that the family does play a role in language interests of the HLL. The family is one of the main reasons why the HLL is in class. Also, when the HLL chooses to learn a dialect, it is always the dialect used by the family. The HLL almost always mentions that family as the reason to learn the language, usually one of two reasons is given: to communicate with extended family or to make the parents proud.

The parents are one of the early sources of language input the learner has; they influence the dialect the HLL learns. When the parents have been away from the local Arabic environment of the dialect, they tend to lose contact and are not up to date with the "newer" vocabulary or expressions that appear with time. This is why often HLLs with advanced dialect speaking skills might sometimes use older language expressions or might not understand the trendier words used by their generation in the Arabic community in the Arab World. HLLs who follow the media, watch movies, and listen to Arabic songs, as well as those who travel on a more regular basis to the home country of the parents, are more up to date and do not face this issue. Yet, not many fluent speakers come to an Arabic class in the university classroom. This is probably because they are above the level of the courses offered in the Arabic language program or they have already learned MSA to the proficiency level they want.

There is no one specific element about the family of the university HLL that has to be present. There are several points to look at when discussing the family, and they can differ. The structure of the heritage speaker's family affects the exposure to the HL, Arabic in this case. At times both parents can be native speakers of Arabic, at others just one of the parents is a native speaker. The presence of extended family members in the home environment who use the HL, and to what extent, is another element that affects proficiency. The social community and the use of the HL within the community are also factors that also play a role in the development of the HL.

The book does not discuss first or second language acquisition of children or bilingual language learning. This is a stage that the HLL has been through before coming to the university class, and it does not have any direct impact on the HLL for the class. It can be said with certainty that the HLL who registers in the university program has not reached a high level of HL proficiency and they do not see themselves as bilinguals, or else they would have been above class level for the university courses. Benmamoun et al. (2013) believe that the majority of HLLs do not reach full HL acquisition.

The reason that the HLL is in the classroom at the university level is because as a child the HLL did not acquire the language to the proficiency level they want. They might have started to learn it, but they never reached the fluent near-native or native proficiency language level. There are different explanations as to why this happened, such as the parents did not have the time to communicate with the learner in Arabic or they felt that they did not want to confuse the child by teaching them a home language. At times, children refuse to speak the HL, which they recognize as the weaker language and they prefer to use the more dominant community language. Even when the HLL speaks Arabic at home but does not go to a formal school to learn the language, they miss out on the literary and formal Arabic with all the additional vocabulary and the more complex structure that they can learn from that context. This is why they later come to learn the language at the university. They need to be placed in a class that meets their language needs and their proficiency level.

A closer look at the HLL and the family of the HLL helps shed light on how this learner perceives the Arabic language. In order to know the HLL, interviews and semi-formal discussions with students were conducted at the end of the semester. This allowed the students to express what they think about the language and what they hope to achieve. They also discussed their proficiency level and what they see as their strong or weak points, which are important when teaching the HLL.

5.4 Understanding different levels of the HLL

The HLLs who comes to learn Arabic at the university are not homogenous and have different levels of proficiency, for both the dialect and MSA. The HLL can be a beginner dialect speaker who hardly ever uses Arabic; they do not use Arabic at home, or they speak minimal dialect on an irregular basis. In this case, the learner has to start learning Arabic from the beginning – like a non-HLL Arabic student. This learner is often seen by the others as a HLL, but in reality, the family did not use Arabic at home, and it would not be possible for this learner to build on any previous knowledge they have.

For the G-HLL who is an intermediate dialect speaker and yet their MSA is not present, this learner cannot take a beginner MSA class with the non-HLL as they will be transferring dialect knowledge into MSA and thus can be quicker to learn at the beginner MSA level. At the same time, they are not a true beginner. This G-HLL sees themselves as a speaker of the Arabic dialect; they can communicate in dialect, but they cannot read or write, and when they listen to MSA in formal contexts they cannot understand it. This group of G-HLLs can usually discuss the topics that are within their everyday usage in dialect. This partly explains why such a learner is easily frustrated in the MSA class, as they are not used to finding themselves unable to communicate in topics out of their daily register and in MSA. The learner can feel awkward and at times embarrassed of their level of Arabic and this affects the learning process; the educator has a key role to ensure that this HLL can overcome their worry and concern over a brief time. The experienced professor can develop a system to help the intermediate dialect speakers overcome that feeling. Several techniques can be used, including allocating individual, one-on-one time with the teaching assistant or the professor, having the learner involved in choosing what they read and write, and creating or adapting activities in order to meet the wants of the learner. It is also important to acknowledge the progress made by the learner as the confidence in MSA is not always present.

In the case of the intermediate and advanced dialect speaker, this learner already has knowledge of a dialect, and the MSA material the learner studies should build on that and not ignore the dialect that the HLL already knows. As the Arabic language material does not cater to the HLL, the professor has to guide the learner and has to use supplementary, in-house material that will help the individual HLLs in the class. Based on the dialect the HLLs speak, the professor can develop worksheets that make the shift from the dialect to MSA smoother and quicker. These worksheets can include pronunciation exercises where the shift in phoneme pronunciation from the dialect to MSA is practiced. Another successful grammar worksheet, for example, would explain and practice how the negative changes from the dialect to MSA and how the prefix or the suffix is used to show the negative in dialect is not the same as the prefix used for MSA. At times, the G-HLL mainly needs the professor to tell them that you change the dialect pattern you are familiar with to the new MSA pattern you are learning in class.

The purpose of an intensive beginner MSA class is to give the HLLs the base that allows them to succeed in studying MSA. The frustrations and successes the learner experiences should be analyzed in order to allow the language educator to make use of the positive points and avoid the mistakes with future HLLs. For instance, the confidence level of the learner changes throughout the course, with the progress in MSA. This is seen in the group activities where the HLL usually starts to contribute more to the discussion or when there is a change from being a silent observer to the willingness to participate in answering questions or reading aloud in class. The following step is the participation in class discussions and then, later, volunteering to give examples. Recording the progress of the HLLs throughout the course to find out if there is a pattern, or stages, these learners go through ensures that in the future, professors are better equipped to answer the needs and wants of this level of HLLs.

Professors often consider HLLs as false beginners in MSA. Actually, HLL dialect speakers are false beginners with insufficient language input. The only input they have is the dialect input that they acquired in the home environment, and they have minimal or no formal learning of MSA, which native speakers have when it comes to MSA. It can be argued that even the uneducated native speaker is exposed to MSA through listening to it in the media or reading the newspapers and other publications. The HLL has incomplete exposure to the Arabic language,

82 *Heritage language learning pedagogy*

and this is why they are in class. Educators need to look at the learner who communicates in dialect and build on what the learner knows. Individual variation, language placement, skill development, and learner needs and wants all play a significant role in getting the learner to an intermediate level of MSA.

There are a number of questions that need to be answered about the HLL and the role of the family. There is no research to answer these questions. First, how can the dialect a HLL speaker brings to class help them to learn the language; and can this knowledge that the learner brings to the learning situation be used to help make a shift to learning MSA. The information presented here is based on the observation of the professors, as well as informal discussions with individual students and semi-structured group interviews with the HLLs at the end of the semester. This aims to describe a "pattern" of HLLs who come to the classroom. It also aims to give a brief outline of the progress the HLLs makes throughout the course – from when they join the beginner Arabic classes, until they finish the intermediate course.

In the following section, different HLLs are introduced to show the different varieties of learners who study Arabic in a university in Montreal, Canada. This aims to give a better understanding of the HLL, how they see the language, and the class. The four learners are meant as a sample of HLLs at different levels of language proficiency; they represent the learners that are always present in the classroom. This also acts as a reminder that the HLL is not always confident about their language skills. The discussions reveal that these learners share common elements, positive and negative. They all want to learn Arabic and are happy with the progress they make, but they also have worries and concerns about the language as they try to learn it. The following section briefly outlines the progress the HLLs goes through when learning MSA.

The next section presents individual students from different levels in order to see how the HLLs are actually different and cannot be seen as one homogenous group. It also helps to show that the different levels that professors see in the class occur not only in one specific situation or place. The four learners presented below have different dialect levels: no dialect, beginner, intermediate, and advanced. They are all beginner MSA students since they did not attend any formal Arabic classes before the one at the university. The HLL coming to the MSA language classroom has acquired knowledge of the Arabic language, mainly in dialect and knows very little MSA. The beginner dialect and MSA student is a student who actually does not need to be assessed to be placed in the class that meets their level. They are a beginner and as such are placed in a beginner Arabic class. For the HLL beginners, it is recommended that they be grouped in one class, especially at the early language levels, if this is feasible from the administrative point (see Section 6.3.3).

5.4.1 G-HLL beginner dialect, beginner MSA

Nour[7] is a first-year, male student born and raised in Montreal, Canada. His family is from Morocco, from an Amazigh Muslim background. When Nour talks about his family, he says that although his father speaks Arabic, he is not an Arab. The family has pride in the Amazigh heritage and does not speak Arabic at home; they understand the language and they know the *Darja* (Moroccan-Arabic spoken dialect). He wants to learn Arabic to connect with the religion and better understand his roots. The family is not ethnically Arab but recognizes the importance of learning Arabic. In the Amazigh language, there are words from Arabic origin, and in the streets in his parents' hometown in Morocco, the language used is Arabic. He chose to come to learn Arabic and continued Arabic classes for three semesters.

He came to the Arabic class with basic words of Arabic as well as with cultural understanding and an obvious desire to learn Arabic. As a learner, he was always asking questions about the language and how it works, and he tried to make sure he understood correctly. He found the class to be a place where he could ask about the culture and the habits of the people in the Arab World. In the informal interview after the end of the semester, he said that one of the positive things about the class was that it made him realize that he is not the only HLL who did not learn Arabic as a child. In his first Arabic class, he found the script difficult to learn, more so than the vocabulary. His pronunciation of the phonemes was not native-like and he needed to work on it. As such he was placed in the Beginner I class, that starts from the beginning of learning MSA. Nour continued to study Arabic and in his third semester he was in a class with non-HLLs. In the intermediate class he continues to ask about the language; he often verifies the cultural information with his father and would come back to class and share what he discussed with his dad in class. It is interesting that this learner finds Arabic to be a link with his father, as well as his family back in North Africa.

5.4.2 G-HLL intermediate dialect, beginner MSA

Joe is a second-year student who is familiar with a dialect (Lebanese) and came to the Arabic class at the university to learn MSA. Due to the diglossic state of the Arabic language, Joe had no knowledge of MSA even though he can communicate in dialect. This learner is an example of a HLL who speaks the dialect at an intermediate level but has no knowledge of the written script or MSA vocabulary and grammar. Joe thought that he needed to start from the beginning and learn all the formal vocabulary, as well as learn the alphabet, and did not consider the dialect to be related to MSA. This can be as true, he is a beginner MSA, but not a beginner when it comes to vocabulary or pronunciation. The possibility of placing Joe in a class that starts teaching the alphabet assures him that he is not "missing-out" on parts of the language.

Concerning Joe's learning of the Arabic script, his handwriting was huge so that he could give himself space to add the dots and diacritics above the letters. His handwriting was similar to young children learning to write in the Arab World. Few learners (HLL or non-HLL) have such big and hesitant handwriting. In class, he was always worried that he did not write correctly, and he once commented saying, "My mom would kill me if I do bad in this course." The role of the mother as a motivator to learn the language is seen in the case of Joe. When asked about his plan to learn Arabic, he said he will continue to work at home with the help of his mother as she was already helping him with the studying and the homework. After Joe finished his first semester of Arabic, where he learned the basics of reading and writing and basic grammar, he did not continue his Arabic classes at the university.

5.4.3 G-HLL advanced dialect speaker, beginner MSA

Sarah is a first-year female student from an Egyptian background. Sarah registered for the HLL class in the Fall semester. She could not read and write, and she did not feel the need to contact the department for placement, especially as there was no department permission required to register for this class. At the very beginning of the course it became clear that Sarah did not belong in the beginners' class. She was an upper-intermediate speaker and even though she could not read and write she needed to move to the intermediate Arabic class. She knew enough Arabic to make an easy shift from dialect to MSA. The only things that she did not have were knowing how to make the shift from MSA to dialect and how to read and write in Arabic.

She had the vocabulary in dialect, and this meant that she needed to learn what words were only dialect and which words could be shifted from the dialect into MSA. Although she could communicate well, her sounds were not always correct and very often Arabic phonemes were mispronounced. Her advanced knowledge of the dialect meant that she could not be placed in a total beginners class, as she would not be learning or improving her proficiency after finishing learning how to read and write the script. She was keen to learn the language and wanted to go to the Beginner II class, where they learn the grammar basics. Since she did not read and write, she could not join, so she waited a semester where she had help from her mother to learn the script before registering in the Arabic class the following semester. It was interesting to see how she continued to seek help from her mother during the following year. She would not hand in a homework with a mistake and would say that her mother had a look at it but did not change anything. She also came to class with questions that she had asked her mother regarding the grammar and her mother did not know the grammatical reason to answer her question. The student was happy to take the answer from the classroom and go and tell her mother the answer, "it is so and so because of this reason." This happened more than once during the semester and the role the mother played was quite noticeable. The student continued taking Arabic for two semesters and stopped at the intermediate level as there was no advanced class offered at the time.

The three students presented above represent the G-HLL group of learners. The majority of HLLs who come to learn the language at the university have minimal or no knowledge of MSA. They have personal interest to learn the language as they have family from the Arab World. Knowing the personal backgrounds of these learners aims to show why they come to the class and what makes them continue learning. This should be taken into consideration when planning classroom activities or developing material. Activities for the HLL should build on these elements, where they develop the skills they need starting from what they have.

5.4.4 M-HLL, writes Arabic script

Yusuf is a second-year engineering student and his family is originally from Pakistan. He is a practicing Muslim and uses the language to pray. He could write the script but had minimal understanding of the words. At the beginning of the class he did not realize that he had a basic knowledge of Arabic that allowed him to be in the Intensive Beginner I class. At first, the class was out of his comfort zone and he felt at a disadvantage to be a M-HLL in a class with Arabic HLL while he was not of Arabic background. This changed within two weeks of the class, as he became aware that the words that he knew in Arabic were in MSA, while the Arabic HLLs knew the words in dialect, which is often not the same. Also, he was already familiar with the script while the other HLLs were not. His participation in class increased and, as the class went on, he became more confident with his knowledge.

Like many of the M-HLLs, he was not as challenged by the MSA grammar rules. He looked for examples that illustrated the basic rules and he found them in his repertoire of vocabulary in MSA, as it is from the religious context. This was usually on the word level, for example when forming plurals (masculine, feminine, or broken) and for understanding the use of diacritics and vowel endings on nouns. At the next level of language learning, both the G-HLL and the M-HLL are at the same level; they both go to the next level of language learning where the language and how it works is all new information and they can take in the same class with the non-HLL.

One last point regarding the M-HLL is that they tend to relate the Arabic language mainly with religion. The learner said in the semi-structured interview that as a child his father would wake him up for dawn prayers and recite the Quran every morning before school. This shows the role the family and the religion play in establishing the importance of Arabic for the M-HLL. Thus, once in class the instructor (non-Muslim) was talking about Islam and the importance of Arabic in the Quran and he happened to present information that contradicted what the learner knew about the language, and the learner was taken aback. Yusuf followed up with the professor individually after class regarding the information and even went to talk to another language professor (a Muslim professor) regarding what was said in class. The point here is that the M-HLL links the language to the religion and even though MSA is not CA, it is still the way this learner takes to understanding the language of his faith and belief. Yusuf took another language class the following semester, and this is where his Arabic classes stopped; but like other HLLs, his relation to the language does not end with the end of the class.

The HLLs discussed here represent the HLLs group of learners in the Arabic language classroom. The next step would be to research more about the needs, lacks, and wants of the HLLs. Research into HLLs is starting, and it is expected that the points that are raised here and the questions asked here will be answered in future research. The HLLs need to be placed in the MSA class based on their language level. If they are fluent dialect speakers, they cannot be placed in a beginner or lower intermediate MSA class. Yet, if they have never studied MSA, then this poses a placement problem especially if the university does not offer different language levels to meet the special needs of these learners.

Notes

1 The hyphen between Muslim-heritage is to establish that this is a language learner who is Muslim; not a Muslim HLL opposed to a Christian or non-Muslim from the Arab World.
2 The MLA is one of the most established organizations that focuses on the study of languages and literatures. It has been established for more than a century and is a resource for many who work in the field of teaching languages. It collects data about the languages that are taught across the US as well as provides other services to language instructors nationwide.
3 https://www.caslt.org/en/general-information/the-association/about-caslt.
4 Edmonton Public School https://epsb.ca/programs/language/arabicbilingual/ retrieved in October 2019.
5 Statistics Denmark http://www.dst.dk/Site/Dst/Udgivelser/GetPubFile.aspx?id=207 03andsid=indv2015 in Nielsen 2017.
6 They use the term ancestral language to refer to a language in the past of the learner; it can be an indigenous, minority, or heritage language.
7 Names have been changed; no real names are used.

Bibliography

Arab American Institute. (2019, October 15). *Demographics*. Retrieved from Arab American Institute Website https://www.aaiusa.org/demographics.

Benmamoun, E., Montrul, S., and Polinsky, M. (2013). Defining an "ideal" heritage speaker: Theoretical and methodological challenges reply to peer commentaries. *Theoretical Linguistics*, *39*(3–4), 259–294. doi:10.1515/tl-2013-0018.

Dhahir, O. (2015). The intercultural aspects of sociocultural-interactive strategies. *Al-'Arabiyya*, *48*, 43–59.

Duff, P. A., and Li, D. (2009). Indigenous, minority, and heritage language education in Canada: Policies, contexts, and issues. *The Canadian Modern Language Review/La Revue canadienne des langues vivantes*, *66*(1), 1–8. doi:10.3138/cmlr.66.1.001.

Iranian Languages (2016, February). Retrieved November 2019, from Encyclopaedia Britannica https://www.britannica.com/topic/Iranian-languages.

Looney, D., and Lusin, N. (2018). *Enrollments in languages other than English in United States institutions of higher education, summer 2016 and fall 2016: Preliminary report*. Web Publication: Modern Language Association of America.Retreived from https://files.eric.ed.gov/fulltext/ED590075.pdf

Looney, D., and Lusin, N. (2019). *Enrollments in languages other than English in United States institutions of higher education, summer 2016 and fall 2016: Final report*. The Modern Language Association of America. Retrieved from The Modern Language Association of America https://www.mla.org/content/download/110154/2406932/2016-Enrollments-Final-Report.pdf.

Nielsen, H. L. (2017). "Arabic-as-Resource" or "Arabic-as-problem"? Arab heritage learners in Danish postsecondary education. In O. Kagan, M. Carreira and C. H. Chik

(Eds.), *The Routledge handbook of heritage language education from innovation to program building [VitalSource Bookshelf version]* (pp. 363–378). New York: Routledge Taylor Francis Group. Retrieved from vbk://9781317541523.

Statistics Canada. (2012, October). *Linguistic characteristics of Canadians*. Ottawa: Published by authority of the Minister responsible for Statistics Canada. Retrieved June 2019, from Statistics Canada https://www12.statcan.gc.ca/census-recensement/2011/as-sa/98-314-x/98-314-x2011001-eng.cfm.

Valdes, G. (2005). Bilingualism, heritage language learners, opportunities lost o seized? *Modern Language Journal, 89*(3), 410–426.

Additional References

Al-Sahafi, M. (2015). The role of Arab fathers in heritage language maintenance in New Zealand. *International Journal of English Linguistics, 5*(1). doi:10.5539/ijel.v5n1p73.

Belnap, R. (1987). Who's taking Arabic and what on earth for? A survey of students in Arabic language programs. *Al-'Arabiyya, 20*(1/2), 29–42. Retrieved from www.jstor.org/stable/43191686.

Cumoletti, M., and Batalova, J. (2018). *Middle Eastern and North African immigrants in the United States*. Retrieved February 2019, from https://www.migrationpolicy.org/article/middle-eastern-and-north-african-immigrants-united-states.

Kheirkhah, M. (2019). Guiding parents towards raising bilingual children. *Special issue: Language, heritage, and family: A dynamic perspective, Issue Editor: Christina Higgins. International Journal of the Sociology of Language, 2019*(255), 159–165. doi: 10.1515/ijsl-2018-2007.

King, Kendall, Fogle, Lyn W., and Logan-Terry, Aubrey (2008). Family language policy. *Language and Linguistics Compass, 2*(5), 907–922.

Melo-Pfeifer, Silvia (2015). The role of the family in heritage language use and learning: Impact on heritage language policies. *International Journal of Bilingual Education and Bilingualism, 18*(1), 26–44. doi:10.1080/13670050.2013.868400.

Montrul, S. (2011). Introduction: The linguistic competence of heritage speakers. *Studies in Second Language Acquisition, 33*(2), 155–161. Retrieved from www.jstor.org/stable/44485999.

Rouchdy, A. (2002). Language conflict and identity: Arabic in the American diaspora. In A. Rouchdy (Ed.), *Language contact and language conflict in Arabic: Variations on a sociolinguistic theme* (pp. 133–148). London: Routledge Curzon.

Valdés, G. (2005). Bilingualism, heritage learners, and SLA research: Opportunities lost or seized? *Modern Language Journal, 89*(3), 410–426.

Van Deusen-Scholl, N. (2003). Toward a definition of heritage language: Sociopolitical and pedagogical considerations. *Journal of Language, Identity and Education, 2*(3), 211–230.

You, C. (2001). Heritage vs. non-heritage Issues Revisited. *Korean Language in America, 6*(275), 284. Retrieved from www.jstor.org/stable/42922786.

6 The heritage language learner and the Arabic language classroom

6.0 Introduction

In this chapter, the focus is on the classroom and the pedagogical environment. The classroom is the learning environment where formal (and informal) learning takes place, and there are several elements that come into play in the classroom such as the professor, the students, and the material. There are also non-classroom factors that contribute to the success of the learning such as the curriculum, type of program, and all administrative and practical components; these elements contribute in the making of a successful language learning course at the university level. In this chapter, the main focus is to share in-class experience and to discuss how the classroom dynamics work in order to benefit from the practical experience of qualified language professors. The successful modifications and alterations that are made by the professors are shown here as they can be a guide to build upon in future teaching. Things that have worked for language professors based on trial and error can be adapted to the different classrooms in different places; points that did not work and/or are annoying in the classroom are presented to see how they can be corrected in order to avoid repeating them.

This chapter looks at the Arabic classroom and it presents a detailed description of an Arabic university course that has been adapted for HLLs. It also discusses an important classroom aspect that has an effect on the language learning process: the pros and cons of having HLLs and non-HLLs in the same class. The chapter gives several examples of students' and teachers' points of view to the points presented in this chapter. The focus is on the implementation and practical aspects of the classroom, not the theory. The last section of the chapter looks at immersion programs, both in the US and in the Arab World, to see how these programs work, how HLLs are placed in them, and how they perform in these programs.

6.1 The language professor and the HLL

A look at the professors of Arabic in Europe and North America will reveal that there has been a number of changes over the last decades. When Arabic was taught in the West in the past, it was usually the CA variety and it was taught by non-native, Western professors. The change in the teaching of foreign languages, in general, from a grammar/translation school to a more communicative approach, has also poured into Arabic. The last decades of the twentieth century saw a move away from focusing on classical texts to more up-to-date texts, as well as a shift toward teaching of Arabic dialect. It also saw a change in the background of the professor of Arabic, who is no longer necessarily a Western professor researching old classical Arabic texts. This continues in the twenty-first century. Professors today include Arabic native speakers, second generation Arabs, as well as English native speakers who have learned both MSA and Arabic dialect.

The background of the language professor is very often questioned by the learners. They always ask the native professors where they are from. In the MSA class, when the HLL cannot find out from the professor's spoken language where they are from, they ask the professor, either during the first class or immediately after the class, about their background. When asking colleagues who teach Arabic, they all agreed that this is a regular question that students have asked. The non-native professors of Arabic are highly qualified, but as Abuhakema points out, "heritage Arabic speakers may not identify with or appreciate a nonnative speaker of Arabic as a teacher" (Abuhakema, 2012, p. 76). In an open-ended discussion with students, they reported that they were surprised and impressed by the knowledge of their non-native professor of Arabic. They were impressed that they not only spoke the dialect fluently, but also could use and explain the formal MSA grammar rules accurately. A closer look into whether or not the language background of the professor affects the learners' decisions regarding the Arabic class would be necessary in order to find out if these observations are the same across the board.

There is no exact data available to give exact figures about the number of professors of Arabic and their backgrounds, but a look at the American Council on the Teaching of Foreign Languages (ACTFL) annual meeting reveals how there is now a larger number of American university professors teaching languages such as Arabic and Chinese than there was a decade ago. Also, there appears to be more job openings for language professors at the university level every year, which indicates that more classes are opening and there is a need for qualified professors. The presence of both native and non-native professors of Arabic in language groups on social platforms reflects the changes the field is witnessing.

The professor has different roles, and these should not be overlooked. Professors are seen differently by the students, the colleagues, and the administration. Professors are seen by the student to represent a power in the classroom because of the decisions they take when it comes to pedagogy and managing the class (teaching methods, tests, and exams). Also, they are a source of knowledge on different levels: academic, cultural, social, as well as linguistic (Dhahir, 2015). The student has expectations from the professor; they trust that the professor recognizes their language level and can help them build on what they know. For the HLL, this means that the professor should be able to address the individual case of the specific HLL who usually has a larger dialect vocabulary than the non-HLL, but lacks formal MSA grammar rules; this requires qualified professors, who are a rarity, as Abuhakema (2012) points out.

90 *Heritage language learning pedagogy*

The professor of Arabic has multiple roles to play in order to succeed in their teaching mission. The professor is seen by the student as the teacher, the facilitator, and the organizer of learning tasks in the classroom, as well as the examiner at the end of the course. There is no one-and-only way to deal with learners in general, or with HLLs in particular. As such, the professor will have, at times, to adapt the teaching style to what they see best for a given group of learners. In intermediate classes and above, one way to make students exchange information and communicate is to have both a HLL and non-HLL do the pair and group work together. This has the advantage of having the students discuss and explain to each other how they have come to an answer. It also allows for all the learners to use their Language Learning Strategies (LLS) and benefit from the different experiences they have (see Section 6.2). This is where the professor can organize the class so that students always have time in class to do the activities. This allows the professor to monitor from a distance, support, and step in to explain or correct a point, but only when asked by the students. There are times when the HLL can be a support for the non-HLL, and there are other situations where the HLL needs to be guided into following the system of the class and not get carried away on a separate path as some HLLs tend to do. At the end of the day, HLLs have come to the class to learn Arabic.

The second role the professor plays is that of a colleague. An important point to look at is the dynamics and coordination between colleagues within the same language program; this is very important as it reflects upon the success of the program. If the program has more than one professor, then coordination between colleagues is an essential step in building the program. Newly established programs usually start with one professor and grow with time. Coordination helps develop the required consistency of the program and ensures that the positive learning experience the learner has does not change with the change of professor in different courses. This is why it is recommended that the policy toward HLLs, for example, be agreed upon among colleagues in the same program. The same way students share their learning experiences with each other when it comes to courses, professors should share teaching experiences with colleagues in the form of regular professional meetings and workshops. They are expected to follow the same strategies when it comes to placement and evaluation of the HLL, or choosing course material and testing, for example. The policies they follow should be agreed upon and supported by the department administrators as this ensures smooth running of the language program.

As the world changes, professors and language teachers communicate and exchange ideas through the new channels available, as well as the traditional ways. Thus, while conferences, workshops, and seminars are available and are used widely, new means of exchanging ideas are emerging as well. The use of social media, such as Facebook groups, dedicated to a specific academic or applied field of study or work, is becoming more common; teaching Arabic as a Foreign Language (TAFL) is no different. Facebook has a number of groups dedicated to TAFL, and more continue to appear. Facebook is an open platform for teachers to exchange ideas, comment on what works in the classroom and what does not, discuss how to improve on the teaching and classroom management, as well as share any other points of concern or interest. This, at times, is a support for a small language program since the professor now has virtual colleagues with whom they can discuss the pros and cons of whatever professional ideas or issues and exchange ideas and experiences with. What is interesting is that members are from all over the globe: the US, Canada, Australia, United Kingdom, Denmark, the Arab World, and more. The participants can be native speakers or advanced proficient speakers of Arabic who have chosen a career in this field. They can post practical questions or academic and reflective points for professional discussion. Such groups are relatively new, but the number of participants, whether posting points for discussion or commenting and answering, is increasing regularly, which means that they are seen to be a useful tool by those in the field.

What is very useful is the fact that the response can be immediate and the feedback about any topic or issue discussed can be as diverse as the members of the group and their different work situations. The social platform also ensures that all members get to know about recent publications, upcoming conferences, or new material and courses being taught in different places. It is an open space for all in the field: both the experienced and the starters in the field can benefit from the exchanges. The newcomers to the field learn from the experience of the more senior professors without even having to leave their computer, and at times this distance allows for questions to be asked that otherwise one might think are trivial or unimportant. The social platform is a place to exchange ideas, learn from the practical experience of others, or even simply vent and share teaching and classroom problems. All topics are open to discussion and more than often colleagues help each other by sharing personal experiences to support their discussions and help their virtual colleagues.

Even though, at times, there is no scientific or academic research to back up the solutions offered by colleagues; their success in the classroom is a valid reason to share them on the platform and is welcomed by colleagues. For instance, in one of the virtual discussions online, advice is given from several colleagues on how to manage HLLs when they appear to have a negative, disruptive impact in the classroom. The suggested answer to overcome this is to plan the class so that there is a variety of activities, to keep the HLLs engaged and hold them responsible in class. This is a practical way out of a situation that has not been researched or measured accurately, but it is the hands-on solution that has been tried by others that was shared to answer the problem was being discussed. The positive thing about the virtual groups is that they help create a sense of belonging to a larger group, which many of the TAFL professors do not have in their physical work environment due to the small nature of their program.

The professor is also part of a larger establishment, in this case the university. The professor has a role as a team player in a department, usually of languages, and has to follow the policy of the department and the institution. At times, this means that there will be decisions that are based on the realistic goals and initiatives of the institute, even if this means that the progress of the Arabic program is delayed. It is important that professors follow the university initiatives and develop their programs based on the general university directions. This helps build a stronger language program (see Section 6.5.3).

6.2 Classroom diversity and Arabic language learning strategies

Observing how both HLLs and non-HLLs interact with one another and how they identify themselves gives information about the language learners and the strategies they use to help in learning the language. After teaching Arabic for a few years, language professors usually come to recognize different types of language learners and become aware of patterns of learners that keep reoccurring. There are variables that affect how the learners progress in the language, but in a setting such as the university classrooms today, professors are encouraged to find out more about the learners in order to give the language learners better learning environments. Most of the classes today in Europe and North America are multi-cultural – where the learners come from different places. They have learners who are studying in their home countries, who come from other Western countries, as well as HLLs and other non-Western, foreign, international students.

This diversity in cultural backgrounds and linguistic knowledges in the classroom is worth looking at to find out how it affects the classroom. One way is to find out what features different languages have in common with Arabic, and help students connect the language they are learning with their native language or with the English language, if English is the language of instruction at the university. Non-HLLs from non-English backgrounds feel positive when the professor compares their first language to Arabic, as this is a way to establish a bond between the learner and the language.

As the traditional classroom where all learners are from one background is changing, professors and researchers alike are reconsidering how the learners are grouped. In his examination of the Arabic classroom in a university in Denmark, Dhahir (2015) divided the learners into Arabic HLLs, Danish language learners, and other Language Learners (which includes all non-native speakers of Danish who are not from an Arabic background). This division of learners into groups reflects how the professors and the researchers see learners to be distinct and diverse. Denmark receives a diversity of learners: Danish, immigrants, Europeans, and other international students. The diversity in the classroom might not necessarily be seen to the same extent across all European countries and North America but it definitely is present. The first step is to try to understand how these groups interact and to build a connection and a mutual working system between learners so that the diversity in the classroom helps, not hinders, the language learning process.

The diversity in the language classroom effects the learning situation. In order to find out how the presence of the HLL influences the learning strategies of the non-HLLs, Dhahir (2015) examined the social interactive skills the learners used in the Arabic language class. The students were learning Arabic in Denmark and he attempted to look at how far learners take advantage of the different sources of input in the learning environment. He looked at the following as input: the classroom, the learner with HL background, the native speakers in the surrounding environment, as well as the travel experience. The study looked at the social-interactive strategies to find out whether or not the HLL and the non-HLL (including both Danish language learners and other language learners) used the same strategies when learning Arabic. The results show that there is no significant difference in most of the strategies and that they all use them almost equally. One of the results shows different use of sociocultural strategies; more than 80 percent of non-HLLs ask native speakers of Arabic to correct them while only 50 percent of HLLs do that.

Language learners use learning strategies to help them learn a language; these are the thoughts and actions they take to fulfill a learning task (Chamot, 2004). The language learning strategies (LLS) are reported directly by learners and an awareness of these LLS is a useful tool that professors should use when teaching. There are different ways to look at the LLS and the research continues to develop and add new ways to researching and studying them. Based on Oxford (1990), there are six main LLS divided into two categories: direct and indirect strategies. The direct strategies are memory, cognitive, and compensation strategies; the indirect ones are metacognitive, affective, and social strategies. Each one of these six major groups can then be further divided into subgroups to include more LLS. There are different variables that affect how each learner develops these LLS. These variables can be personal or related to the learning environment. Leaners use these strategies differently, and one difference between the HLL and non-HLL is that the first can rely more on the dialect as a compensation strategy when they do not know MSA. Another point, the HLL seems to neglect the direct strategies of memory and studying more than the non-HLL who uses all their LLS. Chamot refers to how the heritage speakers of Arabic and the non-HLL share many of the same metacognitive strategies when learning to speak MSA, as they share the same challenges. Yet, when it comes to listening comprehension, they are unlike the HLL who reports no difficulty and, therefore, reports no use of LLS to identify Arabic sounds (Chamot, 2004).

6.3 The HLL and non-HLL in the classroom

When considering the HLL in the Arabic language classroom, there is a need to also consider the overall pedagogical exchange that takes place: (1) between the HLL and the professor, (2) between the students in class, (3) the teaching material, and other factors that play a role in the learning process. Remember that the learners, HLLs and non-HLLs, want to learn the language and enjoy the process without feeling pressure or threats from colleagues.

To begin with, most teaching Arabic programs do not separate HLLs and non-HLLs in the language classroom. This can be for several reasons. One reason is feasibility – the university does not offer many language classes and it wants the classes to have a larger number of students, so they will not accommodate two separate tracks, one for HLLs and another for non-HLLs. A second reason is the size of the Arabic program; many of the programs are young programs and as such might not be large enough to have separate non-HLL and HLL classes. Then, there is the fact that there is little research to show whether or not HLLs and non-HLLs should be separated in the language classroom. A number of recent studies shows that non-HLLs can benefit from HLLs when it comes to certain aspects of learning Arabic (Abuhakema, 2012; Ibrahim & Allam, 2006; Bale, 2010; Dhahir, 2015). The data available is limited to the situations and class levels discussed and a general, agreed-upon view about this matter has not been established yet. The number of HLLs in language classrooms has recently increased due to the newer settings on the global level that have resulted in a larger number of immigrant Arabs in Europe and North America, and the language classroom is still adapting to this change. At the moment, ALLs are usually not separated based on HL, and beginner MSA students tend to have a large percentage of HLLs – including both G-HLLs and M-HLLs.

For the non-HLL, the HLL can either be a resource or an obstacle. The non-HLL who is not intimidated actually uses the HLL as motivation for learning and an additional tool to help learn Arabic better. They can ask the HLL for the pronunciation of a word or for the correct understanding of how an expression is used. In his interview with students, Dhahir reports that non-HLLs have said that they listen to the HLL in class and that they find these learners a useful source of language input. On a similar note, one of the students in the Beginner I class recently came up to the professor and said that she was quite happy when she overheard two Arabic-speaking students talk in Arabic on campus; she heard and understood the exchange they had about going to eat and where they were going. The sense of achievement she had made her come and report it to the language professor as a sign of appreciation that she had learned Arabic in a short time and was happy to understand a dialogue between two native speakers on campus.

It happens sometimes that a non-HLL has had contact with HLLs for a while, and as such has more confidence in acquiring the language. It is as if they consider that having contact with native speakers is an advantage and they need this advantage to be acknowledged in the classroom by the professor (who represents a language authority, in that case). For example, a French student in Montreal felt that the professor was underestimating her knowledge of Arabic once when they were explaining the different cultural meanings of using the term *habibi* and *habibti* (sweetheart/darling; masculine singular); the student immediately interrupted the professor to "clarify" that she knows that information. She explained, and even seemed to defend her position, about knowing the terms and how to use them by saying, "I am not stupid, half the people where I grew up use *habibi* all the time." She grew up in Southern France in an area where a large Arabic/Maghrebi community lives. This is information that is not part of her language skills but affects her understanding and usage of the language. As the learner is a non-HLL but has come to know a large number of Arabic speakers, and as such has absorbed knowledge about the language and culture in a natural medium, she felt that this is information she had to share with the language professor. This had led her to be confident in her intermediate Arabic class and to benefit from having HLLs in the classroom and not feel threatened by that.

6.3.1 The HLL and Arabic varieties in the classroom

When language learners, non-HLL or G-HLL, ask about the Arabic program, one of the initial questions they ask is which dialect they should learn; they do not ask what level of Arabic they would reach after a semester, a course, or a year. The exception is the M-HLL who is interested in MSA (and CA, which is usually not offered) and because of that does not show interest in learning a dialect. They do not start by asking when they will be fluent users of the language, but they want to know which dialect they should learn, even on their own, if the program teaches MSA only. They want to know which dialect will help them understand and be understood in the Arab World. There is no one correct answer to this question. This is a decision that each program takes based on both the administrative and the pedagogical situation. Arabic language programs differ in their approach to this topic. It usually depends on the size of the program and the number of classes the program offers as well as the dialect spoken by the professors. Programs can offer MSA only, or start with MSA then add a dialect, or start with both varieties at the same time.

The HLL is a different story, they usually know what they want from the language course. The HLL (both the G-HLL and the M-HLL) usually asks for MSA, not the dialect. This can be because the G-HLL sees the dialect as a variety they can learn at home. Their main interest in Arabic at the university level is to become a reader of Arabic. The G-HLL needs to learn how to modify or switch from the dialect to MSA and when to do that. This is a problem area for them as they not do not have any formal Arabic education and the shift from dialect to MSA is an important skill they need to develop (Boussofara-Omar, 2006). The M-HLL needs MSA for the religious role of the language; they do not need a spoken dialect. They have a specific need from Arabic, and MSA is it. In general, it has been noted that HLLs tend to request MSA mainly, while non-HLLs want to learn both MSA and a dialect. This is an area for further research when looking at the HLL in the Arabic language program.

6.4 The HLL and knowledge of Arabic language and culture

The HLLs bring cultural awareness to the class; for example, they are more familiar with Arabic greetings, food, dress codes, and family relations. They confirm what the teacher is saying and often act as a support to what is said in class. It is the case, sometimes, that students can reach out and help each other. They have experienced elements of the culture firsthand; for example, the HLL has probably seen their parents receive guests, and observed the tradition of offering food to a guest, and what is natural to them needs explanation to the non-heritage learner. Most HLLs tend to offer to explain to their colleagues these unfamiliar cultural concepts. They also have the benefit of being able to compare to the Western culture they live in. Often a HLL would get enthusiastic and carried away by sharing with the class cultural points such as Arabic hospitality and eating habits when guests are at the house in an Arabic environment as opposed to the Western culture. At other times their recognition of cultural points is seen by a nod of the head or smile of the face. This allows the HLL a moment of "cultural success" where they can connect to the HL.

It is generally agreed upon that the HLL may have command of the dialect and knowledge about the cultural behaviors before entering the language classroom. It has been noted, for example, that the HLL has more knowledge of forms of address that are used in formal situations in Arabic. Arabic is a language that uses special pronoun-like form of address instead of the regular "you" for respect when addressing specific people in formal contexts generally such as when addressing an older person. This form of respect is also seen when using a title before the name of the professor, for example, and not simply using the first name. Non-HLLs might not be aware of that, and at many universities in North America, professors can be addressed by their first names. Most of the HLLs will not be addressing the professor using the first name, or without a form of address such as Miss/Mr./Professor or Doctor. This is a point non-HLLs might not be aware of; the forms of address in Arabic follow a tighter code than they do in English, particularly if the language professor is clearly a generation older than the students. In this case, very few (if any HLLs) will use the first name to address the professor. It is interesting to note that the many non-HLL will tend to mostly follow the HLL when addressing their professor.

The HLL who registers for Beginner I Arabic is usually a student who has no familiarity with the written script or has learned it as a child at a weekend school for a limited time and has never gone back to it. What the HLL is not cognizant of is that they know more Arabic than they are consciously aware of. This comes in different forms; it can be familiarity with the meaning of the name or with basic vocabulary that their parents have been using randomly. When it comes to the language, the HLL may have never learned MSA, but knows that the language is written from right to left and that the Arabic alphabet connects letters to each other. They can identify an Arabic script, even if they cannot read or write that script. They know that there are two language varieties, i.e. diglossia. They have heard MSA on the news and can recognize that MSA is different than the dialect used by the family members. HLLs will probably know that there are Arabic sounds that are not found in English and vice versa, and they might even know that diacritics (symbols placed above the consonants) act as short vowels in English. The familiarity to the written script will vary. On the grammar and sentence structure level, depending on the frequency of Arabic use at home, they can be familiar with grammatical structure such as the imperative, the question forms, or the simple past in Arabic as there is a chance that they might have heard these structures growing up in a house where Arabic dialect is spoken.

On the speaking and pronunciation level, most of the Arabic HLLs tend to have less problems with the phonology of the language. They can hear, recognize, and distinguish Arabic sounds quicker than the non-HLL. As Arabic has phonemes that are not present in the English or French phonology, the non-HLL needs more time to distinguish the phonemes than the HLL. Also, HLLs can pronounce the Arabic phonemes quicker than the non-HLL. This means that they will need less time practicing and learning the correct pronunciation. Also, they have had exposure to the dialect, and even though their listening skills are good, their speaking skills are at times very weak. They use English to communicate with their family members but understand the Arabic dialect to a certain extent. This is what makes it complicated. The differences between the G-HLL and M-HLL need to be indicated and analyzed to see where they meet and where they differ. It is true that not all HLLs can be grouped together in one class; background and language proficiency are elements that are looked at when placing learners in the classroom.

HLLs tend to feel obliged to "know it all" and always want to know the answer; they cannot see themselves making mistakes. When they do, as any language learner, they tend to laugh at themselves for making a "silly" mistake that they should not have made. This sense that they should know it all can be a problem and can affect their classroom participation. Often, they do not want to be caught making language mistakes, when they should know the language. They know the dialect and, as such, fall into the trap of assuming that they will not make mistakes in MSA. This is seen when they come to read MSA and they mispronounce a phoneme or add the wrong case ending to a word. These areas of language learning are problem areas for HLLs such that they will not admit to. This often means that they choose to be quiet in class to avoid making mistakes, even if this means missing out on practice and learning.

6.5 The HLL and the Arabic coursebook

The earlier trends in teaching Arabic have focused on, and stressed, the teaching of reading and writing. There was little emphasis given to speaking and listening in MSA. This later changed and an integrated approach has been encouraged by a number of researchers. The integrated approach includes teaching a dialect for speaking and listening in the same class, not just MSA skills. The goal is to have a learner proficient in the four skills; and in order to achieve native-like proficiency, learners have to learn a spoken dialect. The question that needs to be looked at now is whether to teach MSA and dialect in separate classes or to teach both simultaneous in the same class. There are advocates for both trends and arguments that support or refute the integrated approach of both in the same class.

There is a noticeable pedagogical shift in Arabic teaching toward spoken language. Arabic educators are increasing their use of spoken Arabic in the classroom to reflect real-life situations. The material for teaching Arabic has changed and developed. For instance, the Georgetown series *Al-Kitaab fi Ta'allum al-'Arabiyya – A Textbook for Teaching Arabic*, first edition 1995 (Brustad, Al-Batal, & Al-Tonsi, 2011) and the preliminary text of the series introducing the alphabet *Alif Baa'* (Brustad, Al-Batal, & Al-Tonsi, 2010) both adopted a basic integrated approach from the very beginning and at the time this was quite a new approach for learning for TAFL. The second edition added a colloquial section at the end of each unit and the third edition had two varieties (Cairene and Damascene) integrated into the units with less and less MSA (Wilmsen, 2017). In a perfect world where the teaching hours are available, one option to consider is having separate track MSA and dialect classes. This way the students learn both varieties. This is what is done in immersion programs or in study-abroad programs (see Section 6.6). For students who are going to a study-abroad program, the separation of MSA and dialect classes is recommended as learning the dialect does help intercultural development (Palmer, 2012). Another series of three books that uses the integrated approach is *Arabiyyat al-Naas*, which translates to *The English of the People*. From the title of the book, one can tell that this book aims at teaching the Arabic language that natives use, whether spoken dialect or written MSA. *Arabiyyat al-Naas (Part One): An Introductory Course in Arabic* (Younes, Weatherspoon, & Saliba Foster, 2013), uses the integrated approach of teaching MSA and Levantine dialect together. It was followed by a second book, *Arabiyyat al-Naas (Part Two): An Intermediate Course in Arabic* (Younes & Al-Masri, 2013) that presents the educated Levantine dialect through cultural topics in 21 theme-based topics. The third part was published a year later, and again maintained the integrated approach. The books are meant to take the learner from the beginner to superior ACTFL level over the duration of a three-year undergraduate program. The integrated approach is recommended for the ALL but the order of teaching the varieties is still a work in progress.

Language books for TAFL are being published more and more nowadays. There are new books coming out every year, as well as new revised editions of existing books. Different programs have different approaches to the material they use. Some programs mix and match from different sources, while others supplement by in-house material that meets the level they are teaching. The in-house material often follows the ACTFL or CEFR guidelines and are designed to help learners reach a specific ACTFL or CEFR level such as intermediate, advanced, or superior.

No material has been tailored for the HLL; this may be because the interest in HLLs is a recent development in TAFL. Another reason may be that this is not a homogenous group of learners and there is a difference in levels among the HLLs, which makes material development a more difficult task. It is a challenge to develop material for this group. One way to overcome that is to develop separate modules that come together to form a course, where there are different modules, or separate units, to go with the different levels of the HLLs. Also, to have separate modules for G-HLLs who use the same dialect; this can be used when there is a large group of G-HLLs in a particular program. Another useful material build-up tool is the use of worksheets, or a workbook. These can be developed for certain aspects of the language that the HLL needs additional help with. Material for HLLs is a large project and will need the collaboration of an experienced group of material designers and writers to ensure that the modules fulfill their goal and answer the needs of this specific group.

6.6 University undergraduate curricula

Most of the university undergraduate courses offered in major universities in North America and Europe offer beginner and intermediate classes of Arabic language, as well as literature and/or culture courses; they can also offer a Minor in Arabic Studies. A good percentage of these universities offer advanced Arabic with a Major or a BA in Arabic, and a smaller group of universities offer an Arabic graduate program. Like any language program, there are usually more beginner classes than advanced or graduate classes. The beginner classes are more popular among students as language learners very often start to learn a language as an elective course and stop after the introductory level. Another reason for the fewer number of advanced and graduate courses is that students often do not take the language class when they start their undergraduate program, but in their second or third year. Thus, they are graduating before they can finish the higher-level language courses in the university. The academic year can be divided into semesters or quarters, but the duration remains the same – students can learn the language for four or eight months a year, plus summer. When these students come to take a university language course, they are placed in a class based upon their knowledge of this language. The European languages frequently taught are French, Italian, German, and Spanish and they all use the Latin script, similar to English. As such, the language classes do not teach writing script, since the students already know it.

From the language education perspective, it has been suggested that HLLs and non-HLLs should follow different curricula, as both learner groups process and learn languages in different ways (Son, 2017). Language courses are usually based on the level of Arabic the learner knows. In the case of Arabic, due to diglossia, this can be tricky with HLLs. A practical issue would be that the number of HLLs would not allow for two completely separate classes. One way to solve this false-beginner problem in the case of Arabic is for the beginner introductory class to be divided into beginners for HLLs and a regular beginner class. The HLLs' beginner class will be an intensive or fast-track class, where the course starts from the beginning to ensure that all the learners have the same basic knowledge and to ensure that all learners are at the same proficiency level of MSA in grammar, vocabulary, and writing. The oral and listening skills are a part of the program where HLLs are usually better than non-HLL, so the intensive class will move quicker when teaching these skills.

6.6.1 Description of an Arabic program

Depending of the size of the language program and other practical matters, decisions regarding the program have to be made. In this section, an Arabic program taught in the Languages Department in a well-established university in Montreal, Canada is outlined. It is taken as a case-in-point that represents Arabic programs across Canada, which in turn is a sample for courses in the West. Parallels can be drawn from this program that can be applied to other language programs in colleges and universities in the West. In this language department, MSA is taught as one of the languages offered in addition to Chinese, German, Italian, and Spanish. This program teaches MSA only and no dialect. The Arabic program is a relatively young program in an established university that has an average of 100 students in three levels every year. The program offers a Minor in Modern Arabic. A placement test is available online for all these languages, and a learner with previous knowledge of the language has to take it. The main difference between Arabic and the other languages (with the exception of Chinese) is the fact that the other languages use the Latin script, while Arabic uses the Arabic script, which is not taught at schools in Canada.

The first Arabic language course the learner takes is an eye opener to a new world, a new script, and a new set of rules regarding languages. The Arabic section introduced changes to the program and to the curriculum in order to accommodate HLLs' needs. This was done for better classroom management as well as to improve learner achievement. Canada is a mosaic of different cultures and backgrounds, and the students are a clear representation of this mosaic. The introductory classes have three main groups of learners: non-HLL, G-HLL, and M-HLL. To have these groups in one class at the MSA introductory level creates an imbalance. The total beginners can be intimidated, and feel they are in the wrong place. The Arabic G-HLLs students feel that they should know more but can feel limited and trapped in their dialect. The third group, the M-HLLs, can be seen as a unique group of language learners not seen in many other foreign language learning situations. They are not usually aware of how much Arabic they actually know. They have been using Arabic for religion since early childhood. Most of them know the script so they can write Arabic but cannot understand it. Add to that that they can pronounce the Arabic sounds. They do know a number of words because of the religion, but they very often repeat the words without understanding what they mean. The G-HLL and the M-HLL groups could be together in the same beginner MSA class because they have more common ground with each other than the non-HLL group. The two groups share elements that will permit them to work together in class, but their knowledge is not identical and they both share the knowledge of the phonology, for example.

At the university level, before the academic year starts, students register online for their courses – including language classes. The Arabic program offers the following language classes: Beginner I, Beginner II, and Intermediate I classes. Classes above that level are not currently offered on a regular yearly basis. The Minor in Modern Arabic is designed so that the student can finish the Minor in two years. Total beginners can register in the Beginner I class without contacting the department. The learner has to email the Arabic program language administrator to get department permission to register in Beginner II and Intermediate I, since they already know "some" Arabic. Beginner II and Intermediate have the Beginner I course as a pre-requisite, so no department permission is necessary. This allows students to register immediately and not wait for the department permission, but it also allows for misplacement of learners; learners who should register in Beginner II but could register in Beginner I if they have never studied MSA. This means that students from an Arabic background, i.e. HLLs with no formal knowledge of MSA, also register in the Beginner I class with the non-HLLs.

To resolve this issue the Arabic section faculty discussed the possible ways to manage the problems of placement, as HLL misplacement was a recurring matter.

The situation was analyzed to find the cause of the problem; is it the student, the program, the administration, or a combination of more than one factor? The decision was reached that the way to solve this is multi-leveled, and it involves both the professors and the department administrators. Three changes were to be made: first, to add a total beginner MSA class for the HLL. Second, it was agreed to have oral assessments for HLLs with no written knowledge of Arabic. The final change was the administrative change, this included having changes made on the university website to help HLLs find the correct class for them, as well as changes to the record system for students registering for the Arabic program. This process did not happen all at the same time, and it was revised and refined after each step was taken. The final changes included adding an intensive beginner MSA class for HLLs at the Beginner I level, as well as conducting more oral interviews and meeting with students to assess their true language level.

The solution to have two separate classes for the Beginner I classes was implemented: one for non-HLL and another for the HLL. The non-HLL, regular class and HLL fast-track both start from the very beginning and cover the same MSA material. The HLL Beginner I class meets for two hours and a half of MSA a week while the non-HLL class meets for five hours of MSA a week. The faculty agreed to use the same material in both beginner classes, as the students come together as one group in the following level. This works well, and by the end of the course the students are all expected to be at a similar level. They can start the second level from the same point, the basics are covered, but in two different classes. This gave the professor time to focus on the specific needs of each group. For example, more time is spent on pronunciation of certain letters with the non-HLL group than with the HLL group. Also, more class time is allocated to the manual process of writing and how to move the pen on paper to write correctly. Meanwhile, for HLLs, the influence of dialect on MSA is evident, and in this case the teacher has to guide the learners to make a transition from the spoken variety to the more formal MSA pronunciation and vocabulary.

6.6.2 Curriculum changes and administration

There are two sides working together in the university to ensure the success of the educational purpose: the academic and the administrative. The latter often imposes guidelines or restrictions on the academic side for practical, non-pedagogical reasons. This is why, when working on language planning, even on the smaller departmental level, the changes proposed need to be approved and supported by the university. In some cases, this means that the academic has to look at the "selling point," or the positive addition, that the administration would find in the proposed changes so that it supports them. The administrative hierarchy starts from the department up to the senior university administrators and, depending on the type of change, it might need official government approval – in the case of adding a Major in Arabic studies, for instance. The department administrators, the student advisors, and the faculty and university administrators have to approve and support the changes.

The changes with the new placement process have been quite positive on all levels and have left the language professors and the administrators satisfied with the results. On the administrative level, the beginner classes have higher enrollment, as the HLL has a separate class and the intermediate HLL takes a placement before the academic year begins. This way the university avoids having students drop after one or two classes, leaving places vacant. For the last three years, the HLL class has filled up and the university understands that it was a move in the correct direction from the administrative perspective. Another important point to consider when proposing changes to the university is the cost. Regarding proposed curriculum changes, they will be more quickly approved if they do not require additional budget costs. In the case of this course, it is one that would allow more students to register in the Arabic program and would result in an increase in student numbers, which can be built upon as it allows for future growth of the program.

The addition of the course resulted in better classroom management for the professor. It was evident that the students were better grouped. There were no more complaints from students about the different levels in class, or homework being too difficult for some students and too easy for the others, or any other similar problems. The same material is used in both classes, as students are expected to come together in one group at the following level. Now that both groups have taken the first language course to bring them to the same language level, they can all start the second level from the same point. Also, one other positive result is that the limited number of students who might have come for easy credits now have to work for the grades; the easy class is no longer an option, so they no longer came to register for the class. Thus, the professor had less problems with students coming above class level. Classes are better leveled, and fewer students change from class to class during the first two weeks of school. This has resulted in a much more successful Arabic language class.

6.7 Study-abroad programs and the HLL

Study-abroad programs enable students to experience life in a new country while studying; if they are learning a new language then a study-abroad program gives the learners a chance to have first-hand experience of the language, the culture and life. Arabic study-abroad programs started back in 1944 with the establishment in Beirut of the British Institution the Middle East Centre for Arab Studies (MECAS), and in 1967, the Center for Arabic Studies Abroad (the CASA program) was established in Cairo (Wilmsen, 2017). MECAS closed its doors in 1978 due to logistical and financial reasons; CASA closed its doors in 2011 due to security concerns. It relocated to Jordan for a couple of years and reopened in AUC in the 2015–2016 academic year (American University in Cairo, n.d.). The program in the American University of Beirut (AUB) was seen as an option for students to finish their study abroad in 2011 (Wilmsen, 2017). There are also more recent study-abroad programs based in language institutes in different Arab countries such as in Oman, Jordan, and Morocco. These institutes receive students from different American universities as well as independent students from Europe and North America for study-abroad programs. Not only is there a noticeable increase in the number of Arabic study-abroad programs, there is also an increase in the numbers of students participating in these programs. The Institute of International Education reports that in 2010–2011 there were 8,281 students studying in the Middle East and North Africa (including in Iran and Israel). The numbers dropped after the Arab Spring in 2011 to 6,349 students in 2013–2014 (Institute of International Education, 2019).

Another program that is considered one of the established Arabic language study-abroad programs is the AUB program. As Wilmsen (2017) explains, the Arabic language program in AUB has a summer program and a semester or year-abroad program. The year-long program has separate MSA and Spoken Lebanese classes that are scheduled to allow the students to take both, in addition to their graduate courses, if they are doing a Masters. They can take from six to ten hours a week, as well as take courses with native speakers in areas such as Arabic literature if they want. The summer program is more intensive, with six hours of Arabic a day and around 12 students in a class. Wilmsen adds that a

> large influx of heritage learners – students of Lebanese or Arab background – [are] pursuing study abroad, some wishing to improve their command of the dialect of their parents and in-country relatives and others hoping to enhance their command of the language of writing.
>
> (2017, p. 143)

There are two common forms of language programs to consider here: study-abroad programs in Arabic-speaking countries or immersion programs in non-Arabic speaking countries. The study-abroad program takes place in the Arab World, while immersion programs can take place in North America or Europe, and the students are in as close to an Arabic environment as possible. Short duration immersion programs usually are summer programs that run from six to eight weeks at language centers in different countries across the Arab World, from Morocco to Oman. Several programs in the US offer local immersion programs; these Arabic programs attempt to ensure that Arabic is upheld at all times. Some programs even have the learner sign a language pledge, for example, to only speak the Arabic language throughout the course. Learners also stay in dorms with the professors and are exposed to Arabic throughout the day in the class as well as in activities outside the class. The Middlebury Language School, in Vermont, is one of the key language learning institutes that offers such an immersion program. It has language programs in 11 languages, not just Arabic (Middlebury Language Schools, n.d.). There are Arabic language institutes opening in Europe as a division of institutes in the Arab World located in a safer region, but with the same qualities and experienced native-speaker professors.

Over the last two decades, the US has started to focus more on "critical languages" including Arabic. There appears to be a political need to have speakers of Arabic who can understand, communicate, and translate the Arab World linguistically and culturally. Hence, the State Department invested in language learning programs, inside the US and abroad (US Department of State, 2006). The Flagship Program is one of the programs that started in 2002 as an attempt to have advanced language education in Arabic (as well as in Korean, Russian, and Chinese). Currently, there are seven universities across the US that are part of the Flagship Program (The Language Flagship, 2013). Students study in the US and then they spend one year in the Arab World. Previously they had a choice between Egypt or Syria, but currently the only year study-abroad is only offered in Morocco. After the Arab Spring, and with the turbulence that followed, a shift in the locations of these courses took place. The majority of the programs were in Egypt and Syria, where the Egyptian and the Levantine dialects were taught hand-in-hand with MSA. Yet, many of the American programs that were based in Egypt and Syria have now relocated to other places. Middlebury Schools Abroad relocated from Alexandria, Egypt to Amman, Jordan. Similarly, the American Flagship program relocated from Alexandria, Egypt to Meknes, Morocco.

One of the main points in favor of a study-abroad or an immersion program is that the learner is immersed in the language and the culture all the time, inside and outside of the classroom. The programs are an attempt to provide the learner with total immersion in the Arabic language and culture, which will ultimately lead to higher proficiency levels in the language. Yet, Trentman (2018) points out that the research does not necessarily support this common assumption. Trentman explains that the little research in this field has looked primarily at the oral proficiency using the ACTFL testing system, OPI, to show improvement. She points out that the present information gathered is not sufficient as it does not look into the cases where students do not improve or when the improvement is minimal, and in that case the global nature of the OPI does not reflect the improvement. There is research that shows development of intercultural competence on an Arabic study-abroad program.

Before students go on a study-abroad, there is often an official orientation in their home country. At other times, students seek to learn about where they are going from friends, colleagues, or professors. Trentman (2018) reports that the quality of the study-abroad is as important as the quantity of exposure to Arabic. As she points out, research looking at proficiency and achievement in study-abroad programs looked at how the quality of input and the roles of both social networking and identity influence the students in the programs. Social networking revealed that the small, well-knit group is an indicator of better achievement, and the bilingual native speakers are another positive source of positive language proficiency.

As for identity, it is interesting how a number of studies show that the students became more nationalistic after a study-abroad, as they became more aware of their own racial and ethnic identity (Trentman, 2015). For instance, the Caucasian students experienced being a minority for the first time – this can be positive or negative. Awareness of one's identity is not only during a study-abroad; Dhahir (2015) reported the same finding regarding the Danish students in his study. They felt like a minority in the classroom even though they were studying in Denmark, but the diversity in the language classroom gave them a feeling of being outnumbered. Gender and religion also become factors affecting the opportunity to learn the language; at times it is not as easy for women to interact and find social circles for their language practice as it is for men. There is a certain expectation from the local environment based on gender. Regarding religion, the M-HLL encounters issues that are two-fold: on one hand there is a greater sense of community than what they have in the US and, on the other hand, they are expected to have certain beliefs regarding matters of life that the host society expects from them, which they often do not have. This can cause an uncomfortable feeling after the initial welcome they receive. When discussing the HLL of Arabic, Trentman (2015) notes that the HLL in Egypt feels welcome when they arrive, but with time, they become uncomfortable with how their American identity is not taken into account at times. They also report that they can be mocked because their Arabic skills are not to the level that native speakers expect. Almost all HLL want to return to the location of the study-abroad again in the future. It is as if the journey has made the Arab World more accessible and they have connected with their heritage.

The success of study-abroad programs cannot go unnoticed and they continue to develop and grow in different places. At times, it can be seen as a reward for learning a new language or connecting back with the roots of the learner. Overall, there have been more and more independent students traveling on studies abroad mainly to complete the experience of learning the Arabic language.

6.8 The heritage language learner of Arabic: A summary

Early in the book, what is meant by a HL is presented in order to define the grounds that the following chapters cover. An overview is presented of the Arabic language in an attempt to present a clear picture of the different paths of life from where the HLL of Arabic can come from. This overview covers where Arabic is spoken, what varieties are used, as well as outlining the sociolinguistic levels of the language. ALLs at the university level are increasing every year, and the HLL has come to be present in almost every Arabic language class. There is no accurate data at the moment regarding the number of HLLs or their specific needs or wants. This is an area that needs to be studied in more detail in the future.

The book takes a detailed look at HLLs and divides the HLLs of Arabic into two distinct groups: G-HLL and M-HLL of Arabic – this reflects the reality seen in the Arabic classroom. Each group has its own reasons, background knowledge, and understanding of Arabic. The two HLL groups share a personal heritage related to Arabic, but it is not the same and as such their target goal for learning the language is different; they will each use it differently. This is an addition that aims at better defining the HLL. Not all HLLs are the same in their needs, lacks, and wants. The background of the HLL, the role the HLL plays in the classroom, as well as expectations they have from the language classroom are all presented. This distinction between two groups of HLLs is a starting point, and further research is needed to see where these two groups meet and where they depart.

To date, textbooks have not taken the HLL's knowledge about the language into account. The information they have from the dialect can be seen to help learn MSA, as noted in Chapter 6. The next step is to have materials developed based on this knowledge of the G-HLL. Materials that meet the needs of this learner are in demand, and there is room for developing courses and material to answer them. Language professors often develop in-house worksheets for the learners or rely on their experience to adapt the present material used in the classroom, but this should change in the future. Overall, both HLL groups come to learn MSA, but they have different motivations and reasons for learning MSA, as explained earlier. The integrative teaching methodology, where MSA and dialect are taught hand-in-hand, can work for the non-HLLs as they want to learn a dialect, but for the HLL this does not appear to be what they want.

It is expected that teaching material will continue to develop and more tailored material to meet specific groups of students will be among this material, hopefully. For the HLL there is a need for short, skill-specific, multi-level workbooks as well as course books to cover the needs of this target group of learners.

Placement of HLLs in language classes and measuring proficiency are another area where work is needed. Guidelines for Arabic proficiency need to be more detailed and take into account the dialect, as well as MSA. The dialect of the HLL can either help or hinder as such tools need to be developed to help the HLL make a shift from the dialect to MSA. One further area of research is the upper intermediate or advanced G-HLL who comes to the Arabic classroom; their needs similar or different. SLA is opening the doors to the study of HLs and HLL, and more studies regarding the different aspects of Arabic as a HL are needed in order to give a complete picture for TAFL. The road to study HLLs and SLA is only at its beginning; there is a need for studies in the areas discussed to further develop this field.

Bibliography

Abuhakema, G. (2012). Heritage and non-heritage language learners in Arabic classrooms: Inter- and intra-group beliefs, attitudes, and perceptions. *Journal of the National Council of Less Commonly Taught Languages*, *12*, 73–106.

American University in Cairo. (n.d.). *Prestigious Arabic study-abroad program back at AUC*. Retrieved October 2019, from The American University in Cairo 100 Years https ://www.aucegypt.edu/news/stories/prestigious-arabic-study-abroad-program-back-auc.

Bale, J. (2010). Arabic as a heritage language in the United States. *International Multilingual Research Journal*, *4*(2), 125–151.

Boussofara-Omar, N. (2006). Neither third language nor middle varieties but diglossic switching. *Zeitschrift für Arabische Linguistik*, *45*, 55–80. Retrieved from http://www.jstor.org/stable/43525795.

Brustad, K., Al-Batal, M. & Al-Tonsi, A. (2010). *Alif baa: Introduction to Arabic letters and sounds third edition*. Washington, DC: Georgetown University Press.

Brustad, K., Al-Batal, M. & Al-Tonsi, A. (2011). *Alkitab fi ta'alum al-'Arabiya: A textbook for beginners* (3rd edn.). Washington, DC: Georgetown University Press.

Chamot, A. U. (2004). Issues in language learning strategy research and teaching. *Electronic Journal of Foreign Language Teaching, 1*(1), 14–26.

Dhahir, O. (2015). Studying Arabic as an additional language together with Arab heritage language learners: The intercultural aspects of sociocultural interactive strategies. *Al-'Arabiyya, 48,* 43–59. Retrieved from www.jstor.org/stable/44654038.

Ibrahim, Z., & Allam, J. (2006). Arabic learners and heritage students redefined: Present and future. In K. Wahba, Z. Taha & L. England (Eds.), *Handbook for Arabic language teaching professionals in the 21st Century* (pp. 437–446). Mahwah, NJ: Lawrence Erlbaum.

Institute of International Education. (2019). Retrieved from Open doors report on international educational exchange https://www.iie.org/opendoors.

Middlebury Language Schools. (n.d.). Retrieved from https://www.middlebury.edu/language-schools/languages/arabic.

Oxford, R. (1990). *Language learner strategies: What every teacher should know.* Boston, MA: Heinle and Heinle.

Palmer, J. (2012). Intercultural competence and language variety on study abroad programs: L2 learners of Arabic. *Frontiers: The Interdisciplinary Journal of Study Abroad, 22,* 58–83.

Son, Y. (2017). Toward useful assessment and evaluation of heritage language learning. *Foreign Language Annals, 50*(2), 367–386.

The Language Flagship. (2013). Retrieved January 2019, from https://thelanguageflagship.org/content/flagship-history.

Trentman, E. (2015). Arabic heritage learners abroad: Language use and identity negotiation. *Al-'Arabiyya, 48,* 141–156.

Trentman, E. (2018). Study abroad Arabic programs: issues of concern, research, and future directions. In K. Wahba, L. England & Z. A. Taha (Eds.), *Handbook for Arabic language teaching professionals in the 21st century, Volume II* (pp. 151–161). New York: Routledge.

US Department of State. (2006, January 5). *National security language initiative.* Retrieved April 2018, from https://2001-2009.state.gov/r/pa/prs/ps/2006/58733.htm.

Wilmsen, D. (2017). Arabic as a foreign language at AUB History and current trends. In K. Wahba, L. England & Z. Taha (Eds.), *History and current trends handbook for Arabic language teaching professionals in the 21st century, Volume 2* (pp. 141–150). Mahwah, NJ: Lawrence Erlbaum.

Younes, M., & Al-Masri, H. (2013). *Arabiyyat al-Naas (Part Two): An intermediate course in Arabic.* London: Taylor and Francis.

Younes, M., Weatherspoon, M., & Saliba Foster, M. (2013). *Arabiyyat al-Naas (Part One): An introductory course in Arabic.* London and New York: Routledge.

Additional References

Abdalla, M., & Al-Batal, M. (2011). College-level teachers of Arabic in the United States: A survey of their professional and institutional profiles and attitudes. *Al-'Arabiyya, 44/45,* 1–28. Retrieved January 15, 2020, from www.jstor.org/stable/43208721.

Alhawary, M. (2013). Arabic second language acquisition research and second language teaching: What the teacher, textbook writer, and tester need to know. *Al-'Arabiyya, 46,* 23–35. Retrieved January 15, 2020, from www.jstor.org/stable/43195545.

Coleman, J. A. (2013). Researching whole people and whole lives. In C. Kinginger (Ed.), *Social and cultural aspects of language learning in study abroad* (pp. 17–46). Philadelphia, PA: John Benjamins.

Facchin, A. (2019). *Teaching Arabic as a foreign language: Origins, developments and current directions*. Amsterdam: Amsterdam University Press. Retrieved from www.jstor.org/stable/j.ctvjsf64g.

Ibrahim, Z., & Allam, J. (2006). Arabic learners and heritage students redefined: Present and future. In K. M. Wahba, Z. A. Taha & L. England (Eds.), *Handbook for Arabic language teaching professionals in the 21st century* (pp. 437–446). Mahwah: Lawrence Erlbaum Associates.

Institute of International Education. (2019). Open doors report on international educational exchange. Retrieved from www.iie.org/opendoors.

Kim, H. (2001). Issues of heritage learners in Korean language classes. *The Korean Language in America*, 6, 257–274. Retrieved from www.jstor.org/stable/42922785.

McCarus, E. (1992). History of Arabic study in the United States. In A. Rouchdy (Ed.), *The Arabic language in America* (pp. 207–221). Detroit, MI: Wayne State University Press.

Trentman, E. (2013a). Arabic and English during study abroad in Cairo, Egypt: Issues of access and use. *Modern Language Journal*, 97(2), 457–473.

Trentman, E. (2013b). Imagined communities and language learning during study abroad: Arabic learners in Egypt. *Foreign Language Annals*, 46(4), 545–564.

Trentman, E. (2015). Arabic heritage learners abroad: Language use and identity negotiation. *Al-'Arabiyya*, 48, 141–156. Retrieved from www.jstor.org/stable/44654042.

Vanniarajan, S. (1990). *Language learner strategies: What every teacher should know* by Oxford, R, 1990 [Book Review]. *Applied Linguistics*, 1(1), 116–119.

Wahba, K. M. (2006). *Handbook for Arabic language teaching professionals in the 21st century, volume II*. Mahwah, NJ: Lawrence Erlbaum.

Wahba, K., & Chaker, A. (2013). Arabic language learning textbooks: An evaluation of current approaches. *Al-'Arabiyya*, 46, 111–123. Retrieved from www.jstor.org/stable/43195549.

Xiao, Y. (2006). Heritage learners in the Chinese language classroom: Home background. *Heritage Language Journal*, 4(1), 47–57.

Xiao, Y., & Wong, K. (2014). Exploring heritage language anxiety: A study of Chinese heritage language learners. *The Modern Language Journal*, 98(2), 589–611.

Younes, M. (1990). An integrated approach to teaching Arabic as a foreign language. *Al-'Arabiyya*, 23(1/2), 105–122. Retrieved January 15, 2020, from www.jstor.org/stable/43194110.

Younes, M. A. (1995). An integrated curriculum for elementary Arabic. In M. Al-Batal (Ed.), *The teaching of Arabic as a foreign language: Issues and directions*. (pp. 233–255). Provo, UT: American Association of Teachers of Arabic.

Younes, M. A. (2006). Integrating the colloquial with Fusha in the Arabic as a foreign language classroom. In K. M. Wahba, Z. A. Taha & L. England (Eds.), *Handbook for Arabic language teaching professionals* (pp. 157–166). Mahwah, NJ: Lawrence Erlbaum.

Index

ABA (American-Born Africans) 6, 7, 9, 10, 12
ACTFL (American Council of Teaching Foreign Languages) 51, 52–56, 58, 61–64, 89, 98, 104
Africa 6, 9, 11, 12, 18, 24, 26, 28, 29, 32, 34–41, 43, 46, 47, 48, 73, 83, 87, 103
Al Arabiya 42
Al Azhar 36
Al Jazeera 42
Al-'Arabiyya 53, 59, 62, 63, 66n1, 66n3
Al-Arabiyya Institute 62
Al-Arabiyya test 62, 63
Al-Kitaab fi Ta'allum al'Arabiyya – A Textbook for Teaching Arabic 97
Amazigh 18, 24, 26–28, 73, 82–83
American Association of Teachers of Arabic 53, 108
Arab American Institute 39
Arab League 18, 25, 26, 28
Arabian Peninsula 20, 21, 23, 25, 34, 36, 37, 45, 73
Arabiyyat al-Naas 98
Arabophobia 44
Aramaic 24, 26
Armenian 26, 27, 29, 58
Asia 11, 18, 32, 34, 36, 39, 46–48, 75, 104
assessment 49, 51, 52, 53–55, 57–59, 61, 63–65, 67, 101, 107

Badawi, S. M. 17, 21, 22
bilingualism 4, 13, 72, 73
Bosnia 34, 45

CA (Classical Arabic) 17, 19, 20, 21, 22, 23, 24, 32, 34, 36, 37, 75, 78, 85, 88, 89, 95
Canada 1, 5, 7, 10, 11, 13–15, 29, 39, 41, 44, 47, 65, 69, 71, 72, 78, 82, 86, 87, 91, 99, 100

Canadian Arab Institute 39, 46n5
CASA (Center for Arabic Study Abroad) 63, 64, 66, 102
CEFR (Common European Framework of Reference for Languages) 51, 52, 58, 59, 61, 62, 63, 98
Center for Immigration Studies 11
Center of Applied Linguistics 7
China 36, 73
Chinese 8, 9, 11, 13, 34, 58, 70, 71, 89, 99, 100, 104, 108
Christianity 5, 31, 54, 56
colonial language 5, 6
Coptic 24, 38

Darja 83
Denmark 41, 43, 69, 72, 91, 92, 105
diacritics 18, 22, 83, 85, 96
diglossia 1, 12, 17, 19, 21, 23, 25, 38, 54, 58, 65, 74, 78, 96, 99

Egypt(ian) 20, 21, 23, 24–28, 37–39, 44, 70, 73, 74, 84, 104–106, 108
Ethiopia 38

Facebook 90
Ferguson, C. 19–22
FLAP (Foreign Language Assistance Program) 8
French 5, 6, 7, 9, 10, 11, 13, 24, 27, 39, 41, 42, 47, 53, 58, 70, 71, 78, 94, 96, 99

Gaza 26
geographical HLL 59, 74
German 6, 8, 9, 13, 18, 19, 41, 43, 53, 58, 62, 70, 71, 78, 99
G-HLL 73, 74, 75, 76, 77, 78, 79, 80, 81, 82, 83, 84, 85, 94, 95, 97, 98, 105, 106

Haj 33, 36, 46n3
Hausa 35

ILR 61, 62, 67, 68
India 5, 7, 13, 14, 28, 30, 33, 34, 36, 37
Indigenous 4, 5, 7, 8, 10, 11, 13, 14, 15, 86
Indigenous Languages Act 10, 11
Indonesia 36, 37, 47, 48, 61, 73, 75
Interagency Language Roundtable Test 61
Islam(ic) 20, 21, 24, 29, 30, 31, 32, 33, 34, 35, 36, 37, 38, 43, 44, 45, 46, 47, 48, 54, 56, 61, 72, 74, 76, 85
Islamophobia 44
Israel 25, 26, 28, 29, 30, 103

koine 20, 28n3
Kurdish 17, 26, 27, 75

LLS (Language Learning Strategies) 90, 92, 93
language policy 4, 7, 8, 10, 11, 14, 40, 46, 79, 87, 90, 91
Latin 9, 15, 18, 26, 29, 35, 37, 38, 65, 70, 78, 99, 100

Malta 37, 38, 45
Maltese 25, 37, 38, 46
Mennonite 8
M-HLL 23, 69, 74, 75, 77, 78, 85, 95, 97, 100, 105
Middle East 17, 18, 19, 27, 29, 40, 43, 46, 48, 102, 103
minority 3, 10, 11, 12, 13, 14, 17, 18, 24, 25, 26, 27, 28, 29, 35, 36, 73, 77, 86, 104
MLA (Modern Languages Association) 69, 70, 71, 86
Montreal 28, 39, 41, 71, 72, 74, 82, 94, 99
Montrul, S. 3, 15, 77, 86, 87
MSA (Modern Standard Arabic) 12, 19, 21, 22, 23, 24, 26, 30, 32, 34, 35, 37, 52, 53, 54, 55, 56, 59, 65, 69, 70, 73, 74, 75, 77, 78, 79, 80, 81, 82, 83, 84, 85, 86, 89, 93, 94, 95, 96, 97, 98, 99, 100, 101, 103, 104, 105, 106

Muslim 17, 20, 23, 24, 25, 32, 33, 34, 35, 36, 37, 39, 40, 42, 43, 44, 45, 46, 47, 48, 63, 69, 73, 74, 75, 78, 82, 85, 86 *see also* Islam
Muslim World 17, 31, 32, 33, 37, 39, 40, 43, 45, 74
Muslim-heritage language learner 69, 74, 85

Nigeria 24, 34, 35, 47
North America 3, 4, 5, 12, 13, 14, 28, 31, 39, 40, 43, 49, 51, 69, 72, 74, 88, 92, 94, 96, 98, 102, 103
NSLI (National Security Language Initiative) 8

official language 6, 7, 8, 10, 11, 13, 25, 26, 27, 28, 36, 38, 71, 73
OPI (Oral Proficiency Interview) 54, 63, 64, 104
Ottoman 25, 27, 33

Persian 13, 23, 25, 29, 30, 33, 37, 75
proficiency 4, 14, 15, 51, 52, 53, 54, 56, 58, 59, 61, 62, 63, 64, 65, 66, 67, 68, 69, 73, 77, 78, 79, 80, 82, 84, 97, 99, 104, 106

Quran 20, 23, 31, 34, 36, 75, 85

Residential School 7
root system 24

Saudi Arabia 29, 34, 43
Semitic 1, 6, 15, 22, 23, 34, 35, 44, 45, 54
Siwa 24, 27
Siwi 30, 32, 35
SLA (Second Language Acquisition) 3, 14, 17, 21, 79, 81, 82, 85, 92, 101, 106
Spanish 5, 6, 7, 9, 10, 11, 14, 16, 41, 53, 58, 64, 67, 69, 70, 71, 74, 78, 99
study abroad 9, 63, 98, 102
Swahili 32, 41, 42, 55

tanween 23

For Product Safety Concerns and Information please contact our EU representative GPSR@taylorandfrancis.com
Taylor & Francis Verlag GmbH, Kaufingerstraße 24, 80331 München, Germany

www.ingramcontent.com/pod-product-compliance
Lightning Source LLC
Chambersburg PA
CBHW071406290426
44108CB00014B/1707